Workbook
English Phonetic Alphabet

COMPANION TO **CHAPTER ONE** OF ENGLISH IS CRAZY

Copyright © 2009, 2013, 2022 Judy Thompson

Also by Judy Thompson

English Phonetic Alphabet Workbook©
Companion to CHAPTER ONE of *English is Crazy*

How Do You Say?
Pronunciation and Expressions Sound Dictionary

Published in 2012 as *Grass is Black*

Speaking Made Simple
Speaking Course Curriculum©

(PDF Format only)

available from **thompsonlanguagecenter.com**

Backpacker's Guide to Teaching English
BOOK 1 **Cracking the Code** – on Pronunciation
BOOK 2 **Need For Speed** – on Conversation
BOOK 3 **You Don't Say** – on Fluency

ABC Facilitated Reading
An interactive literacy system for teaching reading at home

Workbook
English Phonetic Alphabet

COMPANION TO **CHAPTER ONE** OF ENGLISH IS CRAZY

Judy Thompson
&
Noreen Brigden

All rights reserved.

This work is the intellectual property of the author. This book contains material protected under International and Federal Copyright Laws and Treaties. Any unauthorized reprint or use of this material is prohibited. No part of this publication may be reproduced, distributed, or transmitted in any form or by any means, including photocopying, recording, or other electronic or mechanical methods, without the prior written permission of the publisher, except in the case of brief quotations embodied in critical reviews and certain other noncommercial uses permitted by copyright law. For permission requests, email: **judy@thompsonlanguagecenter.com**

Thompson Language Center
Niagara, Ontario, Canada

www.**ThompsonLanguageCenter**.com
email: judy@thompsonlanguagecenter.com

Published by Thompson Language Center, 2022
Developed in Canada

Workbook — English Phonetic Alphabet (powered by English is Crazy)
Published by Thompson Language Center, 2022
ISBN: **978-0-9812058-1-6**

Copyright © 2011 2013 and 2022 by Judy Thompson
Copyright © 2011 original idea by Judy Thompson
English is Crazy is a registered trademark.
English is Crazy, Fourth Edition 2022: ISBN: 978-1-7781823-0-3
(Original title: English Is Stupid ISBN: 978-0-9812058-2-3)

Special discounts are available on quantity purchases from Amazon.

NOTE: If you have received a copy of this document and have not paid for it, please remit $25 US to **judy@thompsonlanguagecenter.com** through PayPal or etransfer. Any unauthorized copying of this copyrighted book in either print or download version, will be subject to prosecution to the full extent of the law.

Every effort has been made to trace ownership of all copyrighted material and to secure permission from copyright holders. In the event of any question arising as to the use of any material, we would be pleased to make the necessary corrections in future printings.

Edited by Noreen Brigden and Ontario ESL Teachers at Island One, Stoney Lake
Clipart by: Art Explosion Image Library CD-Rom Portfolio
Text design by: Noreen Brigden
Cover design by: Gillian Stead
Cover photography by Donna Brown
Layout and Production by: McCorkindale Advertising & Design

Printed in USA

For the teachers who asked for it.

Acknowledgments

Many thanks to:

Noreen Brigden; John Denison; Monica Long; Ayden Young; Karen Lee; Mary Wuergler; Geraldine, Sofia, and Jorge Albanez; Pat and Des Hall; Lydia Aeillo; Beth Ellis; Sandy Leppan; Alexander Harasymiw; Carol Adams; Kim Saniga; Judith Lott; Gillian Stead; Sue Breen; Chris McCorkindale; Katrina Meyer; Al and Helen Anscomb for their help creating this book.

And to:

The Ryans; Morgan, Collin, and Logan; Brennan, Ayden and Rick... just because.

PREFACE	15
HOW THIS BOOK WORKS	16
LEGEND	17
INTRODUCTION	19
THE ESL TELEPHONE ALPHABET	20
THE PAGE THAT WILL SAVE SOMEONE'S LIFE!	21
Instructions for *What's Your Name?*	22
BINGO RULES	24
Telephone Alphabet Bingo Word List	25
DIAGNOSTIC READING PASSAGE	31
Cry Wolf	32
CHAPTER ONE	33
CONSONANT SOUNDS	34
Consonant Sound Formation	35
EPA – 24 Consonant Sounds	36
Sister Sounds	37
LISTENING SKILLS INSTRUCTIONS	38
Teacher's Copy – Sister Sounds 1	39
Sister Sounds 1	40
Sister Sounds 2	41
Hot Tip for Part One	42
Modifying the Exercise for Lower Levels	42
Sister Sounds Suggestion Sheet	43
Consonant Blends	44
Asian Combo	46
Final Consonants	47
Listening and Speaking Skills Template	53
CONSONANT HUNT	54
Food	55
Clothes	56
Body	57
Consonant Discrimination – Advanced	58
Terrible T – Advanced	59
THE WEDDING OF GRAMMAR AND PRONUNCIATION	60
Plural **s**	60
What Sound Does the Final **s** Make?	61
Singular/Plural	62
Pronunciation Rules	63
Past Tense of Regular Verbs – Basic	64
Past Tense Regular Verbs – Advanced	65
MYSTERY WORD MATCH SERIES	66
Words that Start with /b/ – Basic	67
Words that Start with /d/ – Basic	68
Words that Start with /g/ – Basic	69
Words that Start with /h/ – basic	70
Words with /j/ in them – Advanced	71
Words that Start with /kw/ – Basic	72
Words that Start with /m/ – Basic	73
Words that Start with /n/ – Basic	74

- Words that Start with /p/ – Basic 75
- Words that Start with /r/ – Basic 76
- Words that Start with /v/ – Basic 77
- Words that Start with /w/ – Basic 78
- Words that Start with /y/ – Basic 79
- Words with /z/ in them – Advanced 80
- Words with /Ch/ in them – Advanced 81
- Words that Start with /Sh/ – Basic 82
- Words that Start with /TH/ – Basic 83
- Words with /Ng/ in them – Advanced 84
- Words with /Zh/ in them – Advanced 85

CONSONANT SOUND MAZE 86
- Instructions 86
- /b/ – Basic 87
- /d/ 88
- /f/ – Advanced 89
- /k/ – Advanced 90
- /l/ – Basic 91
- Words that Start with /m/ – Basic 92
- Words that Start with /n/ – Basic 93
- /r/ 94
- /Th/ – Basic + ... 95
- /Th/ – Basic + ... 95

THE *SILENT CONSONANTS* RIDDLE – BASIC 96
THE *H* RIDDLE – ADVANCED 97
INVISIBLE CONSONANTS 98
BINGO RULES 99
- Basic Consonant Bingo Word List 100
- Tricky Consonant Bingo Word List 101

FLY SWATTER GAME – WHAT'S THE SYMBOL? 107
CONSONANT SILLINESS 108
CRY WOLF 109

CHAPTER TWO 111

VOWELS 112
- EPA Vowel Formation Chart 113
VOWELS 114
THOMPSON VOWEL CHART 116
- The Most Powerful Speaking Exercise that Ever Existed 117
- Blank Thompson Vowel Chart 118
- Different Ways to Spell the Same Vowel Sound 119
- ESL Telephone Alphabet Colors 120
- Er - Ar - Or Pronunciation 121
- Rhyming Words for Every Color 122

LISTENING SPEAKING SKILLS INSTRUCTIONS 123
- Green /Ey/, Red /e/, Pink /i/ 124
- Gray /Ay/, Black /a/, Red /e/ 125
- White/Pink, Gold/Olive, Blue/Mustard 126
- Purple /Er/, Charcoal /Ar/, Orange /Or/ 127

CIRCLE THE WORDS THAT RHYME 128
- Basic 128

- Advanced 129
- HOMONYM HORRORS 130
- MYSTERY WORD MATCH SERIES 131
  - Gray /Ay/ – Basic 132
  - Gray /Ay/ – Advanced 133
  - Black /a/ – Basic 134
  - Black /a/ – Advanced 135
  - Green /Ey/ – Basic 136
  - Green /Ey/ – Advanced 137
  - Red /e/ – Basic 138
  - Red /e/ – Advanced 139
  - White /Iy/ – Basic 140
  - White /Iy/ – Advanced 141
  - Pink /i/ – Basic 142
  - Pink /i/ – Advanced 143
  - Gold /Ow/ – Basic 144
  - Gold /Ow/ – Advanced 145
  - Olive /o/ – Basic 146
  - Olive /o/ – Advanced 147
  - Blue /Uw/ – Basic 148
  - Blue /Uw/ – Advanced 149
  - Mustard /u/ – Basic 150
  - Mustard /u/ – Advanced 151
  - Wood /^/ – Basic 152
  - Wood /^/ – Advanced 153
  - Turquoise /Oy/ – Basic 154
  - Turquoise /Oy/ – Advanced 155
  - Brown /Aw/ – Basic 156
  - Brown /Aw/ – Advanced 157
  - Purple /Er/ – Basic 158
  - Purple /Er/ – Advanced 159
  - Charcoal /Ar/ – Basic 160
  - Charcoal /Ar/ – Advanced 161
  - Orange /Or/ – Basic 162
  - Orange /Or/ – Advanced 163
- VOWEL SOUND MAZE 164
  - Instructions 164
  - Gray /Ay/ 165
  - Red /e/ 166
  - White /Iy/ 167
  - Pink /i/ 168
  - Olive /o/ 169
  - Olive /o/ 169
  - Blue /Uw/ 170
  - Mustard /u/ 171
  - Brown /Aw/ 172
  - Purple /Er/ 173

- Domino Instructions 174
  - Dominos /Ay/ to /o/ 175
  - Dominos /Uw/ to /Or/ 176
    - Blue, Mustard, Wood, Turquoise, Brown, Purple, Charcoal, Orange 176
- Bingo Rules 177
  - Vowel Bingo Word List 178
- Fun with Vowel Sounds 184
- Cry Wolf 185

CHAPTER THREE 187

- Transcriptions 187
  - Line Match – Basic 188
  - Line Match – Advanced 189
- Transcription Treats 190
  - fUwd/ f o o d – Basic 190
  - klOwz/ c l o t h e s – Basic 191
  - bodEy/ b o d y – Basic 192
  - numbErz and komun wErdz/ 193
    - n u m b e r s a n d c o m m o n w o r d s 193
  - skUwl wErdz/ s c h o o l w o r d s 194
  - envIyErment/ e n v i r o n m e n t – Advanced 195
  - medikul/ m e d i c a l – Advanced 196
  - wErkplAys/ w o r k p l a c e – Advanced 197
  - Déjà Vu – Advanced 198
- Double Trouble Word Search 199
  - fUwd/ Food 200
  - klOwz/ Clothes 202
  - bodEy/ Body 203
  - frUwt/ Fruit 203
  - vejtubul/ Vegetable 204
  - animul/ Animal 205
  - skUwl wErdz/ School Words 206
  - sIyuns/ Science 207
  - envIyErmunt/ Environment 208
  - medikul/ Medical 209
  - wErkplAys/ Workplace 210
- Line Match 211
  - Grammar Words 211
  - Ordinary Words 212
- Practice Native Speaking 213
- Cry Wolf 214

APPENDIX 1 215

- Language Index 215

APPENDIX 2 216

- Sister Sounds 216

APPENDIX 3 217

- Solutions for Chapter One 217
  - Consonant Hunt – Food 217
  - Consonant Hunt – Clothing 217
  - Consonant Hunt – Body 217
  - Consonant Discrimination 217
  - Terrible T – Advanced 218
  - Singular/Plural 218

  Simple Past Tense of Regular Verbs – Basic 218
  Simple Past Tense Regular Verbs – Advanced 218
  Mystery Match Series 219
  Consonant Sound Mazes 220
  The *Silent Consonants* Riddle – Answers 221
  The *H* Riddle 221
  Invisible Consonants 221
  Cry Wolf Sound Search Consonants 221
SOLUTIONS FOR CHAPTER TWO 222
VOWELS 222
  ESL Telephone Alphabet Colors 222
  Er – Ar – Or Pronunciation 222
  Rhyming Words for Every Color 222
  Circle the Words that Rhyme 223
  Basic 223
  Advanced 223
  Homonym Horrors 223
  Mystery Word Match Series 224
  Vowel Sounds Mazes 227
  Cry Wolf Sound Search Vowels 227
SOLUTIONS TO CHAPTER THREE 228
TRANSCRIPTIONS 228
  Line Match – Basic 228
  Line Match – Advanced 228
  Food – Basic 228
  Clothes – Basic 228
  Body – Basic 228
  Numbers and Common Words 228
  School Words 228
  Environment – Advanced 228
  Medical – Advanced 229
  Workplace – Advanced 229
  Déjà Vu Transcriptions – Advanced 229
WORD SEARCHES 229
  Easy Beginner 229
  Food 229
  Clothes 230
  Body 230
  Fruit 230
  Vegetable 231
  Animal 231
  School Words 231
  Science 232
  Environment 232
  Medical 232
  Workplace 233
  Ordinary Words Line Match 233

REFERENCES 234
 BOOKS 234
 MEDIA 234

THOMPSON LANGUAGE CENTER PRODUCT LIST 240

Preface

English is Stupid®, the six-point guide to spoken English, was released at the Teachers of English as a Second Language (TESL) Ontario Conference in Toronto in December 2009. The book and its principles were warmly received by the English as a Second Language (ESL) community at the event. The following year, Thompson Language Center presented the book, its ground-breaking methodology and the prominently featured ***English Phonetic Alphabet*** (EPA) at thirty-five conferences, universities, radio stations and boardrooms throughout Ontario. Not to make a big deal about it or anything, I was also interviewed on CBC, Daytime television, and if you go to www.youtube.com and search for *Judy Thompson,* there is a 15-minute **TEDx** presentation there. Anyhoo – warmly received was an understatement. By the end of its first year, the principles of ***English is Stupid*** were being taught in sixteen countries around the world.

Everywhere we went teachers loved the commonsense approach to the tricky subject of English pronunciation and shared heart-warming stories about how they incorporated the material into their existing language programs. However, we heard one recurring complaint – *there aren't enough exercises!*

In response to the teachers' pleas, the staff at Thompson Language Center turned their attention to developing two new exercise books to complement ***English is Stupid***. The ***English Phonetic Alphabet*** is such a critical foundation for the whole speaking program for every learner level, from every language background that the EPA warranted its own exercise book. This is it: ***The English Phonetic Alphabet Workbook***.

The other workbook, ***The English is Stupid Workbook***, will include exercises for all six chapters of ***English is Stupid***.

Enjoy,

Teacher Judy

English Phonetic Alphabet Workbook

How This Book Works

When the team (mostly Alexander and I) began compiling exercises for the **English Phonetic Alphabet Workbook**, it immediately became apparent that following the order in **Chapter One** of **English is Stupid** was the most logical way to go. As a general guide, **food**, **clothes** and **body** are the three frequently used topics for basic-level English students. The **environment**, **medicine** and **workplace** are three topics for advanced-level student exercises. Use whatever exercises you want for whomever you want – it's your class.

- Instructions precede exercises including tips on how to modify the difficulty of some tasks.

- Titles provide clues to the style of exercise and include the suggested level of difficulty.

- The page headers indicate the chapter, the topic and the series of exercises.

- Special lists of page numbers for specific exercises for different language groups are assembled in Appendix 1 (page 226) for easy reference.

- The book is illustrated with jokes and riddles, partly for fun, but mostly as tools to train students to develop the abstract thinking skills necessary for true English fluency.

FYI: We were going to call the **English is Stupid** exercise book *Two Sheets and a Rubber Band* because two specific exercises and an elastic band are all it really takes to transform a student's speaking ability. That book was too short to charge anyone any money for, so we padded the process with scads of other exercises that soon became *two* new workbooks.

Before we forget ourselves, the **first** of the two most critical exercises that students need to speak English is found in this book on page 118 – the *Blank Vowel Chart*. The other, called *What and Where* is available as a free download from the website. *What and Where* is part of Chapter 3 in **English is Stupid** and therefore not included in this book.

English Phonetic Alphabet Workbook

Legend

 These stars indicate that there is more information on our website, www.ThompsonLanguageCenter.com or www.EnglishIsStupid.com. It could be a free colour download, video lessons, something from our E-store, etc.

 **Just kidding!** Jokes and riddles to develop students' abstract language skills.

English is Stupid, **page xx** – The page number that the lesson/exercise corresponds to in *English is Stupid* will show in the lower left-hand corner.

FYI – For Your Information

Basic – Focuses on **food**, **clothes** and **body** themes

Advanced – Focuses on **environment**, **medical** and **workplace** themes

Exercise Series
- Bingo
- Cry Wolf
- Listening Skills
- Mystery Match
- Sound Maze
- Line Match
- Word Search

Introduction

This workbook teaches students to hear (distinguish) and say (create) the forty individual sounds of North American English.

 ## The English Phonetic Alphabet

24 Consonants
/b/, /d/, /f/, /g/, /h/, /j/, /k/, /l/, /m/, /n/, /p/, /r/, /s/, /t/, /v/, /w/, /y/, /z/
/Ch/, /Sh/, /TH/, /Th/, /Ng/, /Zh/

16 Vowels
/Ay/, /a/, /Ey/, /e/, /Iy/, /i/, /Ow/, /o/, /Uw/, /u/, /^/, /Oy/, /Aw/, /Er/, /Ar/, /Or/

In this workbook, there are only three chapters with very little text and a plethora of exercises in each. Chapter One covers consonant sounds, Chapter Two is for vowel sounds and Chapter Three practices transcribing spoken to written English and back.

Exercises in the workbook follow the same order as in *English is Stupid*. Some particularly effective styles of exercises are repeated in different sections of the book. There are several complete Bingo games, Mystery Match, Listening Skill exercises, etc. Repeating styles of classroom exercises as well as following *English is Stupid* provides continuity. If you experience difficulty using any of the exercises in the workbook, please check the www.ThompsonLanguageCenter.com or www.EnglishIsStupid.com website video demonstrations or contact judy@ThompsonLanguageCenter.com.

The *ESL Telephone Alphabet* is a bonus feature we are delighted to include in the introduction, which has proven to be a vitally important tool to help students communicate over the telephone.

 If all the letters were invited to a tea party, which letters would be late?
U, V, W, X, Y and Z - they all come after T.

English is Stupid, page 65

Introduction

The ESL Telephone Alphabet

ESL students can dial **911** for emergency help,
but they can't tell the dispatcher where they live!

Talking to strangers on the telephone is so challenging that many English learners won't use the phone at all. Without visual clues from gestures and body language, English is an extremely difficult language to understand when you can't see the person who is talking – even for native English speakers.

The names of several English letters sound similar: *a, k, j* and *b, c, d, g, t*... Native speakers often substitute little words to represent the letters of the alphabet when they need to be absolutely clear about important information. For example, my postal code is *L7J 1G9*. When I tell it to someone over the phone, I automatically say, **L 7 John, 1 George 9**.

This is a great strategy that airplane pilots have used for years, but the *Alpha, Bravo, Charlie*... set of words pilots use are too difficult for ESL students, so Thompson Language Center has developed a new alphabet of ordinary words to help ESL students communicate accurately on the telephone.

 **School Daze**

What is the first thing sea animals learn in school?
Their A-B- Seas

Why were the teacher's eyes crossed?
She couldn't control her pupils.

Why are fish so smart?
They travel in schools.

ESL Telephone Alphabet

One of the biggest challenges for English language learners, is talking on the telephone. Without visual clues from body language, English is difficult even for native English speakers to understand. When native speakers need to be <u>clear</u> giving information over the telephone, they use special words to represent individual letters. Here is a useful tool that uses basic words to help ESL learners spell information over the telephone.

Mr. **S**ingh would be "**S**ummer, **I**ce-cream, **N**umber, **G**oat, **H**ouse"

It sounds silly but that is what native speakers do. Use this list of simple words with your students to help them spell important information.

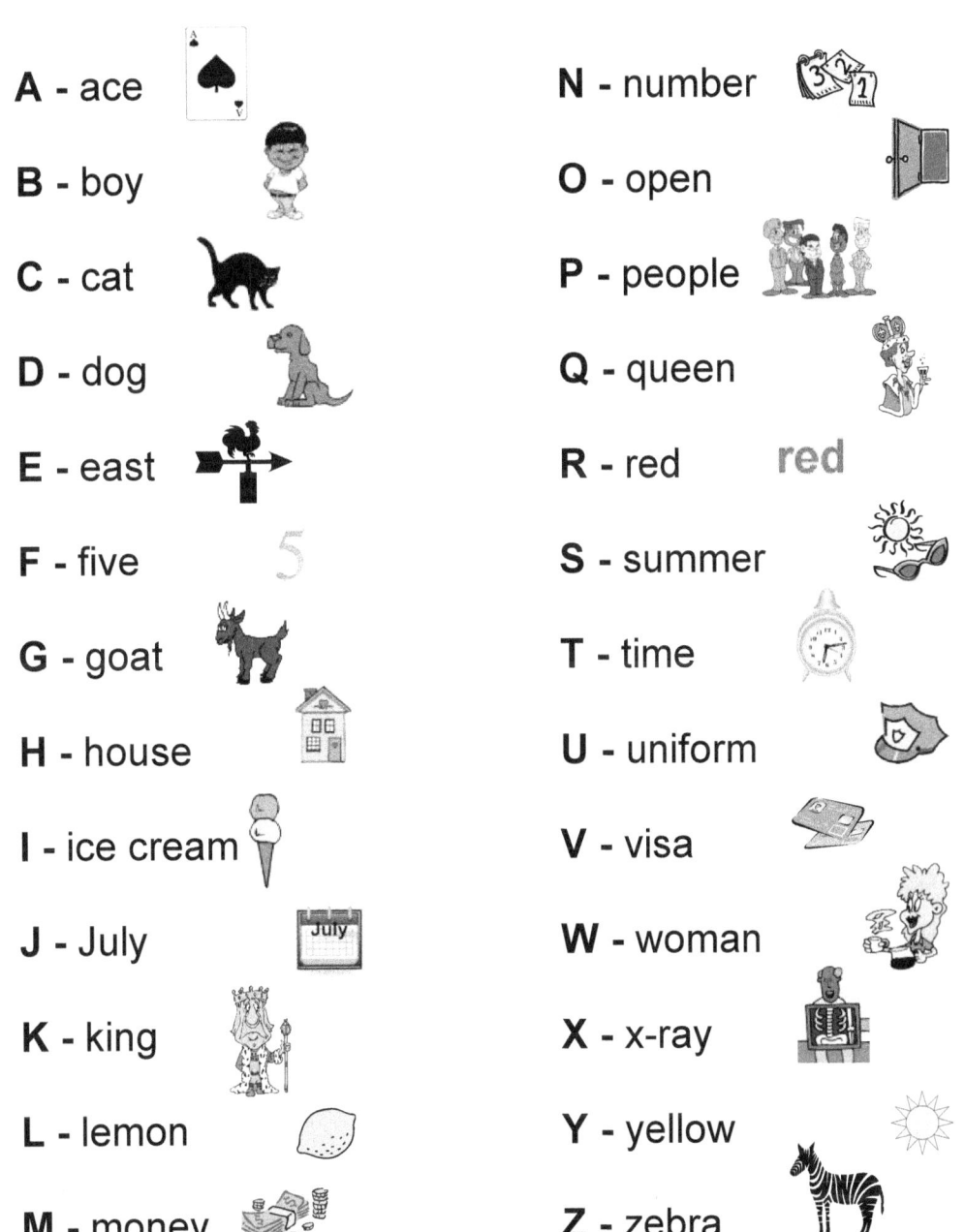

A - ace
B - boy
C - cat
D - dog
E - east
F - five
G - goat
H - house
I - ice cream
J - July
K - king
L - lemon
M - money

N - number
O - open
P - people
Q - queen
R - red
S - summer
T - time
U - uniform
V - visa
W - woman
X - x-ray
Y - yellow
Z - zebra

Introduction

Instructions for *What's Your Name?*

Native English speakers often do this automatically, so it's a matter of bringing to a level of awareness a trick or tool naturally done.

Substitute a simple word representing a letter when spelling over the telephone or in other situations where hearing is difficult.

Have the students create a row of dashes, one dash for every letter in their name. The dashes for my name would look like this:

1. ____ ____ ____ ____
   ____ ____ ____ ____ ____ ____ ____ ____

Then have the students substitute the words from the previous page for the letters of each word.

My name is **Judy**:

J	as in	July
u	as in	uniform
d	as in	dog
y	as in	yellow

Thompson:

T	as in	time	
h	as in	house	
o	as in	open	
m	as in	money	
p	as in	people	
s	as in	summer	
o	as in	open	and
n	as in	number	

What bone will a dog never eat?
A trombone.

Introduction

What's Your Name?
Telephone Skills

Student A: **What's Your Name?**

Student B: **Smith**

        S as in summer
        m as in money
        i as in ice cream
        t as in time
and h as in house

Student A: Smith – S-M-I-T-H

Student B: That's right.

Student A: Where do you live?

Student B: **Brampton**

        B as in boy
        r as in red
        a as in apple
        m as in money
        p as in people
        t as in time
        o as in open
and n as in number

Student A: Brampton – B-R-A-M-P-T-O-N

Student B: That's right.

Student A: Thanks.

Student B: No problem.

Bingo Rules

Students love to play Bingo. Keep a jar of dry popcorn or colored plastic disks on hand as place markers for instant learning fun.

For your own classroom edition of **ESL Telephone Bingo**, photocopy both the *word list* and the *bingo card sheets* on one side only. (A very good idea is to enlarge and laminate the Bingo cards). Cut out the words on the *word list* and drop them into a dark-sided container for the caller to draw. When your class is playing, sketch the four winning Bingo patterns (shown below) on the board for their easy reference

Instructions for the students:

1. Listen for the first letter as the caller calls out a word, so when you hear **summer**, remember the letter **s**.

2. Look to see if you have the letter **s** on your Bingo card.

3. Place a marker over the **s** if you have it.

4. Listen for the *first letter* as the caller continues to call words.

5. Place markers over the letters that appear on your card.

6. Yell out **BINGO**! as soon as you cover the letters in a winning pattern – a straight line going **horizontally, vertically, diagonally,** or one marker in **each corner**.

Good Bingos

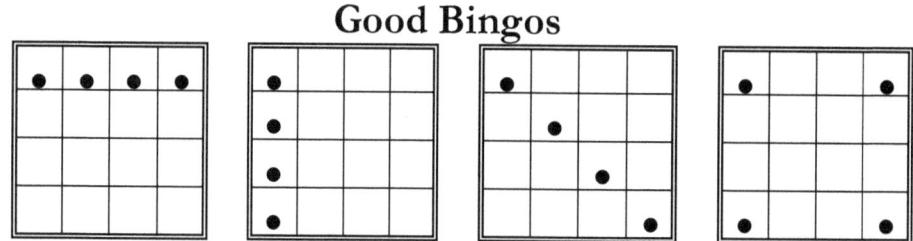

7. Call out the words corresponding to the letters you've marked in your winning pattern.

Congratulations!

The winner then becomes the caller for the next round.

Telephone Alphabet Bingo Word List

apple	number
boy	open
cat	people
dog	queen
east	red
five	summer
goat	time
house	uniform
ice cream	visa
July	woman
king	x-ray
lemon	yellow
money	zebra

 What's worse than finding a worm in your apple?
Finding half a worm.

Introduction — Telephone Alphabet Bingo — Introduction

Card 1

n	s	i	y
l	w	d	o
x	a	j	t
p	h	r	e

Card 2

w	r	s	q
y	z	k	g
p	h	u	d
n	x	f	m

Card 3

v	r	m	l
p	z	a	c
n	g	k	e
t	i	f	b

Card 4

n	x	z	w
m	r	i	j
k	s	g	y
c	q	e	o

How do you keep a rhinoceros from charging?
Take away his VISA card.

© Judy Thompson 2011 — 26 — www.ThompsonLanguageCenter.com

Introduction Telephone Alphabet Bingo Introduction

n	o	q	y
v	c	i	e
u	m	s	h
f	l	k	w

5

w	h	z	f
q	d	g	b
s	j	u	a
m	x	p	i

6

b	x	j	u
h	p	f	m
k	a	z	q
d	w	g	o

7

d	f	z	n
h	v	a	i
j	o	q	m
u	g	y	l

8

What does a cat on the beach have in common with Christmas?
They both have sandy claws.

Introduction Telephone Alphabet Bingo Introduction

x	t	n	i
u	s	r	d
b	g	l	a
v	j	c	q

9

v	d	q	f
e	y	g	k
p	j	t	o
n	c	l	b

10

u	a	m	w
l	f	t	i
e	k	y	h
j	z	p	o

11

s	d	p	w
y	f	q	k
i	t	j	c
b	h	e	v

12

What is a dog's favourite dessert?
An ice cream bone.

Telephone Alphabet Bingo

l	c	p	g
v	n	z	b
d	s	r	w
f	y	t	q

13

w	k	y	u
p	g	z	b
s	l	t	d
r	e	i	c

14

c	g	x	s
d	q	h	b
r	f	u	j
m	o	w	k

15

n	y	h	k
o	a	r	v
p	e	u	x
t	n	l	b

16

What is black and white and red all over?
The newspaper

Introduction · Telephone Alphabet Bingo · Introduction

y	u	a	o
f	z	i	m
n	h	v	x
r	c	l	b

17

x	k	c	i
m	s	v	b
y	a	l	h
t	w	e	o

18

o	a	d	t
e	k	q	p
x	z	c	r
m	v	y	s

19

m	a	v	t
c	i	z	d
o	g	f	j
b	n	e	r

20

 **Why don't zebras like to color?**
They have to stay between the lions.

Diagnostic Reading Passage

Cry Wolf is a diagnostic passage that measures each student's progress over time. The passage helps identify pronunciation of individual sounds that need work. The same passage can be read many times as awareness of certain sound issues are raised. Finally, *Cry Wolf* can be read triumphantly at the end of the book, fully transcribed into the **English Phonetic Alphabet**. Students will be more confident reading out loud when they can see the sounds they are supposed to be making.

Sometimes I employ the Cry Wolf yardstick, and sometimes I don't. It's tough at the beginning because students are embarrassed to make mistakes out loud. It is humiliating for them, and I really don't like that. Trust your instincts as a teacher – the payoff can be worth the pain. To mitigate the student's discomfort, I have the lower levels read the passage privately to me.

For higher levels, it can be a pair exercise. In this case, the date and the names of the reader and the listener go on the page. If possible, the same partner should listen to the reading after every chapter. The students are truly partners in each other's success.

Here's the deal – **until you show them how their first language is interfering with speaking English, they can't make correct English choices. The good news is that each language group usually only makes a few mistakes – the bad news is they make them in every word they say.**

Listen for the Chinese and Taiwanese speakers to clip off final consonants, substitute /s/ for *th*, and pronounce *n*'s as /Ng/.

The influence of East Indian languages has these learners speak too rapidly without any inflection. They enunciate every letter and every syllable equally (English doesn't). This gives their speaking an unintelligible, sewing-machine quality. Typically, Indian speakers substitute /v/ for the letter *w*.

Spanish has fewer vowel sounds than English, so Spanish speakers substitute a long *e* for the vowel sound /i/ and *ship* sounds like *sheep*.

And so on...

    O   Put circles around missing or mispronounced sounds.
    /   Put a slash above words where the inflection is missing.

Date: _____

Reader's Name: _____

Listener's Name: _____

Cry Wolf

Once upon a time, a lonely shepherd boy sat watching his sheep. Nothing unusual ever happened on that quiet hillside, so the boy decided to play a trick on the townspeople. He cried, *Wolf! Wolf! Wolf!* The villagers ran up the hill armed with sticks to drive the wolf away. There was no wolf.

Everyone was angry that the boy was just pulling their leg, but the boy enjoyed his little joke. The next day he cried, *Wolf! Wolf! The wolf is eating the sheep!* Again the villagers ran to help. The boy laughed at them.

On the third day, a big hungry wolf attacked the sheep. The terrified boy screamed for help, but no one came. The wolf ate all the sheep. The boy realized too late the importance of telling the truth.

Comments:

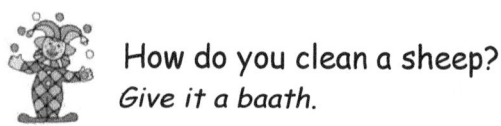

How do you clean a sheep?
Give it a baath.

Chapter One

CONSONANTS

*Brute animals have the vowel sounds;
man only can utter consonants.*

Samuel Taylor Coleridge

Consonant Sounds

What's the difference between a consonant and a vowel?

I was in a course on teaching pronunciation led by Katherine Brillinger when she asked that question. I had no idea – and neither did anyone else in the class.

We knew examples of consonants and vowels, but we didn't know *why*. What makes a consonant a consonant? She said:

Consonants are stopped or restricted sounds.

The Free Online Dictionary entry for consonants looks like this:

> con so nant (kŏn'sə-nənt)
> *n.*
> 1. A speech sound produced by a partial or complete obstruction of the air stream by any of various constrictions of the speech organs, such as (p), (f), (r), (w), and (h).
> 2. A letter or character representing such a speech sound.

I like Katherine's definition better.

At the Thompson Language Center (TLC), we never confuse students with technical mumbo jumbo. I chop the edge of my right hand into the palm of my left hand and say:

Consonants stop. /b/, /f/, /r/ Finished. Consonants stop.

It's the chopping motion more than words that they remember (see the picture on page 33).

Page 35 shows the industry standard style of diagram that indicates where in the mouth and, to some degree, how consonant sounds are created. I must not be a visual person because I have never used this particular tool in a class. But if you would like to use it, here it is.

 What do you get when you cross a karate expert with a pig?
A pork chop.

English is Stupid, page 34

Consonant Sound Formation

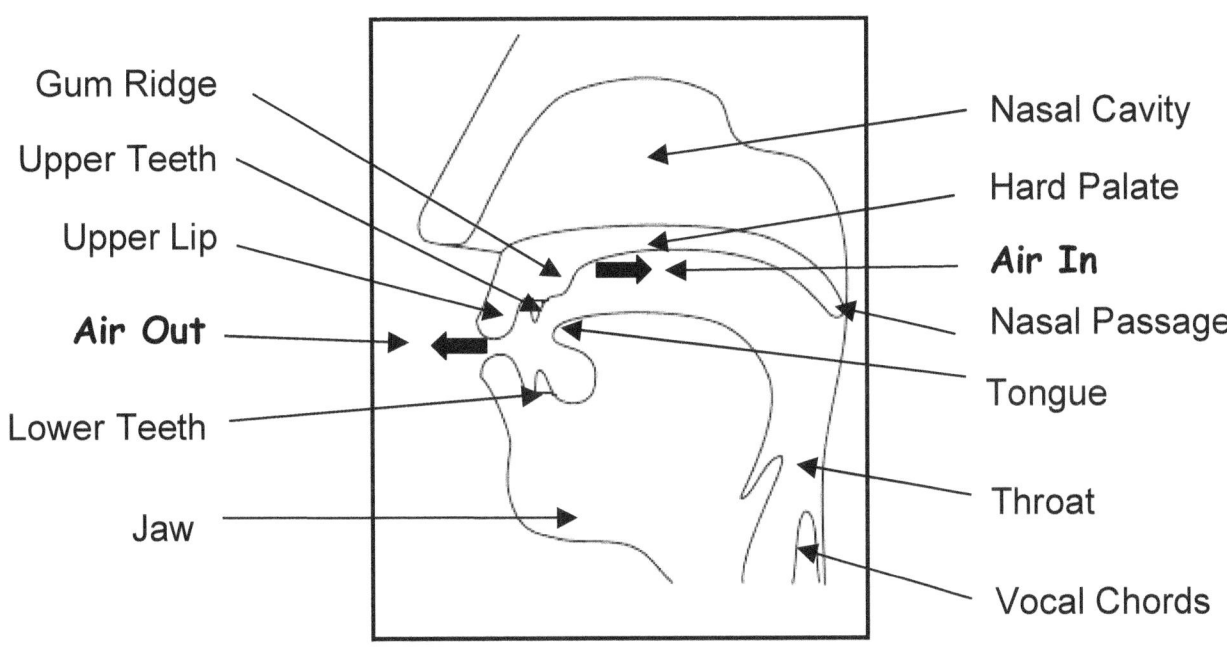

	Both Lips	Top Teeth Bottom Lip	Tongue Between Teeth	Teeth Together	Tongue-Gum Ridge	Tongue-Back Teeth	Teeth Together - Lips Forward	Tongue-Hard Palate	Throat
Breath Stopped & Released	p/b				t/d			k/g	
Breath Constricted		f/v	TH/Th	s/z			sh/zh		h
Breath Stopped & Constricted							ch/j		
Breath Released from Nose	m				n			Ng	
Tongue Touch Up Gum Ridge					l				
Mouth Changes Positions	w					r		y	

 # EPA – 24 Consonant Sounds

18 familiar symbols

EPA Symbol	Key Word	EPA Symbol	Key Word
/b/	boy	/n/	number
/d/	dog	/p/	people
/f/	five	/r/	red
/g/	goat	/s/	summer
/h/	house	/t/	time
/j/	July	/v/	visa
/k/	king	/w/	work
/l/	lemon	/y/	yellow
/m/	money	/z/	zebra

+ 6 new symbols

/ch/	church
/Ng/	Hong Kong
/sh/	shoe
/TH/	think (tongue between your teeth and **blow air out**)
/Th/	then (tongue between your teeth and **suck air in**)
/zh/	Asia, beige, television

= 24 consonant sounds

Beware of **Silent Consonants** – They make no sound. They are everywhere!

thumb, walk, knife, answer, write

Ø is the symbol when a letter is silent.

English is Stupid, page 35

Sister Sounds

Copy the words and the picture from the *English is Stupid* textbook (Appendix 2 on page 214).

To teach people how to speak English, you have to be prepared to make a fool of yourself sometimes. It's part of the job. Most ESL teachers have already experienced contorting their faces, exaggerating sounds and miming like stand-up comedians. Well, this is just another one of those times.

Pinch the top of a regular piece of paper and hold it directly in front of your face. Make the sound **/p/**. Really spit it out, and let your class see the paper move. Now that you have demonstrated, it's much easier for them to be silly too. Tell them to get a piece of paper and do exactly the same thing – **/p/ /p/ /p/** . . .

If the paper doesn't move, they aren't doing it right.

Keep your lips in exactly the same position and draw air in (or *energy in,* as one pronunciation teacher likes to describe it). Make the sound **/b/**. The paper doesn't move.

/p/ and **/b/** are sister sounds (you can see them together on the chart in Appendix 2 on page 214). The mouth starts in exactly the same position. When air is puffed out through the lips, **/p/** is created. If air is drawn in, the sound is **/b/**.

This oversimplified explanation of how sounds are created drives linguists around the bend, but we are not working with linguists. The students need to know how proper English sounds before they go out into the world to put food on their tables – and they are happy with our (TLC) explanation and the results.

There are 8 pairs of sister sounds that cover 16 out of the grand total of 24 English consonant sounds. Sister sounds are particularly difficult for Koreans and languages that make no distinction between /p/ and /b/. The city Busan and Pusan is the same city. Kangnam and Gangnam is the same city...

The Listening Skills Chart Exercise is a fast, effective way for students to hear as well as create these 16 Sister Sounds.

English is Stupid, page 34

Chapter One Listening Skills Consonants

Listening Skills Instructions

We are going to use this style of exercise over and over again because **it's brilliant**. It's a pain in the neck to learn, but **it's soooo worth it.**

The exercise is in two parts. The first part is purely a listening exercise and tunes up the students' ability to hear small sound discriminations. There is a sample teacher's copy on page 39. (Do not give this to the students; their counterpart is on page 40.)

Instructions for Part One (Teacher - columns 1 to 5): Give every student a copy of the exercise found on page 40 and *draw a sketch of the first few lines of the sheet on the board.* Then read this script to your class:

> **I am going to say seven words – *pat/bat* – so you can hear how they sound, then the exercise.** The first entry is:
>
> – *pat, bat* (pause) *pat, pat, bat, bat, pat.*

(They will freak out. **What? What? What did you say? Again, teacher...**)

> **Don't worry! I will say it many times. You are going to get it. When you hear *pat*, put a checkmark on the *top line*. When you hear *bat*, put a checkmark on the *bottom line*. So *pat, pat, bat, bat, pat* looks like this:**

pat	✓	✓			✓
bat			✓	✓	

Check off the boxes on the board as you say the words **pat, pat, bat, bat, pat.**

Most students will understand what they are supposed to do from the demonstration, and they will tell or show those who are still wondering.

At the beginning of the game, say the words seven times to help their listening. Afterwards, repeat the five exercise words (**pat, pat, bat, bat, pat**) a few times – especially for the first few pairs of words because the students are learning to distinguish the subtle differences between Sister Sounds – air out and air in.

This is important: To verify their answers ask, **What did you hear me say?** But they can't say *pat* and *bat* – it is too confusing. Teach them to read their answers using the code **top** and **bottom** according to the positions of the checkmarks. The answer to the first list is **top, top, bottom, bottom, top**. Page 39 is a sample teacher's copy of the exercise followed by the student's copy of the same exercise.

English is Stupid, page 34

Teacher's Copy – Sister Sounds 1

	1	2	3	4	5	6	7	8	9	10	11	12	13	14	15
							Student A				Student B				
pat	√	√			√										
bat			√	√											
pie	√				√										
buy		√	√	√											
time	√			√	√										
dime		√	√												
ten	√	√	√		√										
den				√											
cap		√		√	√										
gap	√		√												
Kate	√	√		√	√										
gate			√												
Sue	√				√										
zoo		√	√	√											
see		√	√		√										
Zee	√			√											
fan	√		√	√											
van		√			√										
thigh				√											
thy	√	√	√		√										
choke	√	√			√										
joke			√	√											
shone	√		√	√											
genre		√			√										

Chapter One   Listening Skills   Consonants

Sister Sounds 1

						Student A					Student B				
	1	2	3	4	5	6	7	8	9	10	11	12	13	14	15
pat															
bat															
pie															
buy															
time															
dime															
ten															
den															
cap															
gap															
Kate															
gate															
Sue															
zoo															
see															
Zee															
fan															
van															
thigh															
thy															
choke															
joke															
shone															
genre															

© Judy Thompson 2011   www.ThompsonLanguageCenter.com

Sister Sounds 2

	1	2	3	4	5	Student A 6	7	8	9	10	Student B 11	12	13	14	15
pest															
best															
pig															
big															
tore															
door															
tuck															
duck															
could															
good															
came															
game															
said															
zed															
sew															
Zoe															
ferry															
very															
fine															
vine															
cheap															
jeep															
chin															
gin															

Hot Tip for Part One
Modifying the Exercise for Lower Levels

Talk in a normal voice at a normal speed. Maybe slow it down a bit for beginners – but not much and not for long. No one is going to slow down for them in real life. This exercise teaches them to *listen faster*. Students suffer for a few minutes at the beginning of the exercise, and then their hearing and ability to distinguish sounds actually improves. This is a skill that will last them for the rest of their lives – a little pain for a big gain!

Part Two (same sheet)

This is a student pair-work exercise for speaking and learning the ability to generate subtle sound differences.

Have the students make check-marks in columns 6 to 10. The checkmarks must be different from the pattern they heard the teacher say (columns 1 to 5), and the checkmarks can't be one above the other.

Random is a good clue word to help support their understanding of the request and you may have to physically help students get started by marking on their page. Put the students in pairs – avoid pairing individuals from the same language group if possible.

The student on the left is Student A and reads first. He/she follows the same routine that you did when you read your list to the class. **I am going to say seven words – pat/bat – so you can hear how they sound, then ...**

She reads the pattern she has marked on her own sheet in columns 6 to 10. Student B checks off the words that he hears and reads the answers back (top, bottom, bottom, bottom, top, or whatever).

Columns 1 to 5 identify their listening issues. Columns 6 to 10 identify their speaking issues. If their partner can't understand what they are saying, the solution is simple – the top words are all air out. Have them exaggerate that. The bottom words in each pair are air in. This is not a trick – the exercise is designed for them to enjoy some real success in these skill areas, and their ability improves immediately.

English is Stupid, page 34

Sister Sounds Suggestion Sheet

Customize the *Listening Skills Chart* for the needs of your class. Here are some suggestions for Sister Sound pairs. A blank *Listening Skills Cart* is available on page 53.

/p/	/b/		/s/	/z/
pack	back		sip	zip
pear	bear		sipper	zipper
pour	bore		sea	Z (USA)
pump	bump		suit	zoot
pest	best			
path	bath		**c**	**z**
			sing	zing
/t/	**/d/**		singer	zinger
to	do		sewn	zone
town	down		sink	zinc
tear	deer			
talk	dock		**/TH/**	**/Th/**
train	drain		throw	though
tore	door		three	thee
			thistle	this'll
/k/	**/g/**		thin	then
coat	goat			
coal	goal		e<u>th</u>er	ei<u>th</u>er
come	gum			
could	good		ba<u>th</u>	ba<u>the</u>
cold	gold		brea<u>th</u>	brea<u>the</u>
clue	glue		tee<u>th</u>	tee<u>the</u>
card	guard		mou<u>th</u>	mou<u>th</u>
coast	ghost			
caught	got		**/ch/**	**/j/**
			cello	Jell-o
/f/	**/v/**		chug	jug
feel	veal		chive	jive
fix	Vic's		chalk	jock
fine	vine		cheer	jeer
few	view		chest	jest
fast	vast		chunk	junk
final	vinyl		char	jar
fuse	views			

Consonant Blends

Side by side consonant sounds or *consonant blends* are difficult for most language groups.

Hot Tip for Consonant Blends

In many languages, consonant sounds are always separated by vowel sounds – but not in English! English has consonant blends like **pl** and **pr**, and they are very difficult for students to pronounce. Here's an easy trick. Find a word that ends with the first sound and another word that begins with the second sound. For example, for **pl**, **sto**p and **l**ight would work. Have the students repeat the word pair more and more quickly – **sto**p **l**ight, **sto**p-**l**ight, **sto****pl**ight – until they are slurred together. Voila! You just got them to say **pl**.

Top **r**ight, to**p**-**r**ight, to**pr**ight – ooh! There's pr...

Here are *Listening Skill* worksheets to practice tricky consonant blends. Feel free to make up your own worksheets using this format and the blank template on page 53.

On page 46, the **Asian Combo** has some consonant blends and some challenging final consonant pairs.

 ### Halloween Hoots

How do you make a skeleton laugh?

By tickling his funny bone

How do you make a witch scratch?

You take away her W.

What is a ghost's favorite fruit?

Boo-berry

Why doesn't anyone kiss a vampire?

Because he has bat breath.

In what language should you write to a ghost?

In Latin – it's a dead language

Chapter One — Listening Skills — Consonants

Consonant Blends

	1	2	3	4	5	Student A 6	7	8	9	10	Student B 11	12	13	14	15
place															
brace															
plaque															
black															
plush															
blush															
fresh															
flesh															
blue															
brew															
bling															
bring															
tree															
three															
stream															
scream															
skunk															
shrunk															
scare															
square															
stress															
tress															
stretch															
scratch															

© Judy Thompson 2011 — www.ThompsonLanguageCenter.com

Chapter One — Listening Skills — Consonants

Asian Combo

	1	2	3	4	5	Student A 6	7	8	9	10	Student B 11	12	13	14	15
play															
pray															
plank															
prank															
glade															
grade															
steal															
still															
green															
grin															
tempo															
temple															
sin															
sing															
kin															
king															
then															
den															
those															
doze															
think															
sink															
word															
world															

© Judy Thompson 2011 — www.ThompsonLanguageCenter.com

Final Consonants

	1	2	3	4	5	Student A 6 7 8 9 10	Student B 11 12 13 14 15

| car |
| call |

| beer |
| bill |

| peer |
| pill |

| wire |
| while |

| ran |
| rang |

| thin |
| thing |

| lawn |
| long |

| sun |
| sung |

| cane |
| came |

| can |
| cam |

| clothe |
| close |

| faith |
| face |

Chapter One   Listening Skills   Consonants

Practicing /l/ and /r/

	1	2	3	4	5	Student A 6 7 8 9 10	Student B 11 12 13 14 15

late
rate

laughed
raft

lead
read

lent
rent

lime
rhyme

list
wrist

load
road

long
wrong

loot
root

lung
rung

loyal
royal

lion
Ryan

Chapter One   Listening Skills   Consonants

/b/ /v/ /p/

						Student A					Student B				
	1	2	3	4	5	6	7	8	9	10	11	12	13	14	15
best															
vest															
best															
pest															
vest															
pest															
berry															
very															
berry															
Perry															
very															
Perry															
b															
v															
b															
p															
v															
p															
brain															
vein															
brain															
pain															
pain															
vein															

Chapter One Listening Skills Consonants

/TH/ /t/

	1	2	3	4	5	Student A 6 7 8 9 10					Student B 11 12 13 14 15				
thank															
tank															
thought															
taught															
thigh															
tie															
three															
tree															
through															
true															
thin															
tin															
with															
wit															
bath															
bat															
tooth															
toot															
both															
boat															
death															
debt															
path															
pat															

Latino Focus

	1	2	3	4	5	Student A 6	7	8	9	10	Student B 11	12	13	14	15
ram															
ran															
some															
sun															
Pam															
pan															
swim															
swing															
ham															
hang															
slam															
slang															
yes															
Jesse															
year															
jeer															
yam															
jam															
old															
hold															
owl															
howl															
o															
hoe															

Chapter One   Listening Skills   Consonants

Hindi /w/ /v/ /r/ – Final /TH/ /Sh/

	1	2	3	4	5	**Student A** 6	7	8	9	10	**Student B** 11	12	13	14	15
wine															
vine															
west															
vest															
we															
V															
whale															
veil															
wage															
rage															
wait															
rate															
wed															
red															
wing															
ring															
path															
pass															
tenth															
tense															
forth															
force															
mouth															
mouse															

© Judy Thompson 2011   www.ThompsonLanguageCenter.com

Chapter One Listening Skills Consonants

Listening and Speaking Skills Template

						Student A					Student B				
	1	2	3	4	5	6	7	8	9	10	11	12	13	14	15

Consonant Hunt

There are 24 consonant sounds in the **English Phonetic Alphabet** found in user-friendly, regular computer keyboard symbols on page 35 of ***English is Stupid***.

24 Consonants

/b/, /d/, /f/, /g/, /h/, /j/, /k/, /l/, /m/, /n/, /p/, /r/, /s/, /t/, /v/, /w/, /y/, /z/ /ch/, /sh/, /TH/, /Th/, /Ng/, /zh/

The following five exercises give students practice in identifying individual consonant sounds in English.

With these exercises, students begin to understand that they can't depend on how words look to figure out how to pronounce them. This switches the speaking software in their brains from visual (reading) to aural (sounds), which helps them develop a new set of tools for speaking English – **by relying on their ears not their eyes**.

There are two big strikes working against the process: brain reprogramming is hard work, and the students' first languages are logical. They really want English to behave in a logical way – **but it doesn't**. Regardless of the students' level of speaking ability, start with basic exercises and let them build on their successes.

Food, clothes, and body are standard themes for the basic exercises; the environment, workplace and medicine are advanced themes. That said – use any exercise you want for any class you want.☺

Lower levels can work in pairs or even small groups to increase their odds of success. **The secret is that they have to say the words out loud**. If someone else says the word, it's easier to hear the sounds the letters are making. We are secretly tricking students into saying more and more English in a safe environment with a strong possibility of success. Students have to get used to the sound of their own voices making English sounds. Their own ability to speak English will grow. It is really only fear that prevents them from speaking – how wonderful to dispel that for them.

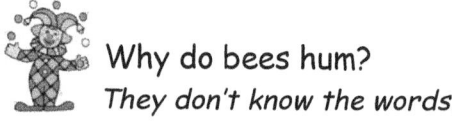
Why do bees hum?
They don't know the words.

English is Stupid, page 35

Food

There are 24 consonant **sounds** in the **English Phonetic Alphabet** and 24 consonant **symbols**. Each symbol is used only once in this exercise. Print the sound symbol for the underlined letter in the slash brackets beside each word. The first one is done for you.

/b/, /d/, /f/, /g/, /h/, /j/, /k/, /l/, /m/, /n/, /p/, /r/, /s/, /t/, /v/, /w/, /y/, /z/ /ch/, /sh/, /TH/, /Th/, /Ng/, /zh/

Hint: Read the words out loud. (Solution is on page 217.)

<u>h</u>am	/ h /	<u>f</u>ish	/ /
<u>r</u>ibs	/ /	corn on <u>th</u>e cob	/ /
<u>v</u>egetable	/ /	mu<u>sh</u>room	/ /
<u>p</u>asta	/ /	<u>t</u>angerine	/ /
<u>c</u>ake	/ /	<u>z</u>ucchini	/ /
brea<u>d</u>	/ /	<u>c</u>elery	/ /
me<u>l</u>on	/ /	<u>ch</u>icken	/ /
<u>y</u>ogurt	/ /	<u>n</u>uts	/ /
<u>m</u>eat	/ /	bro<u>th</u>	/ /
beef au <u>j</u>us	/ /	ca<u>b</u>bage	/ /
<u>t</u>una	/ /	eg<u>g</u>plant	/ /
stri<u>ng</u> beans	/ /	<u>w</u>heat	/ /

What did the fish say when it swam into the concrete wall?
Dam

Clothes

There are 24 consonant **sounds** in the **English Phonetic Alphabet** and 24 consonant **symbols**. Each symbol is used only once in this exercise. Print the sound symbol for the underlined letter in the slash brackets beside each word. The first one is done for you.

/b/, /d/, /f/, /g/, /h/, /j/, /k/, /l/, /m/, /n/, /p/, /r/, /s/, /t/, /v/, /w/, /y/, /z/ /ch/, /sh/, /TH/, /Th/, /Ng/, /Zh/

Hint: Read the words out loud. (Solution is on page 217.)

<u>d</u>ress	/ d /	<u>g</u>loves	/ /
<u>s</u>uit	/ /	lea<u>th</u>er jacket	/ /
<u>c</u>ap	/ /	<u>p</u>ants	/ /
windbreake<u>r</u>	/ /	s<u>w</u>eater	/ /
scar<u>f</u>	/ /	<u>t</u>uxedo	/ /
undie<u>s</u>	/ /	tren<u>ch</u> coat	/ /
<u>h</u>andbag	/ /	<u>v</u>est	/ /
bei<u>g</u>e slacks	/ /	umbre<u>ll</u>a	/ /
<u>u</u>niform	/ /	<u>th</u>ermal socks	/ /
leggi<u>ng</u>s	/ /	<u>j</u>eans	/ /
<u>sh</u>irt	/ /	<u>b</u>riefcase	/ /
<u>y</u>ellow pj's	/ /	<u>m</u>ittens	/ /

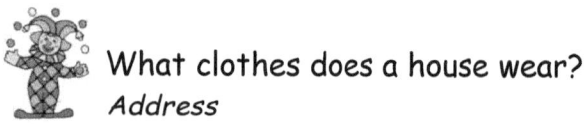

What clothes does a house wear?
Address

Body

There are 24 consonant sounds in the **English Phonetic Alphabet** and 24 consonant symbols. Each symbol is used only once in this exercise. Print the sound symbol for the underlined letter in the slash brackets beside each word. The first one is done for you.

/b/, /d/, /f/, /g/, /h/, /j/, /k/, /l/, /m/, /n/, /p/, /r/, /s/, /t/, /v/, /w/, /y/, /z/ /ch/, /sh/, /TH/, /Th/, /Ng/, /zh/

Hint: Read the words out loud. (Solution is on page 217.)

<u>h</u>ead	/ h /		s<u>p</u>ine	/ /
<u>b</u>ack	/ /		e<u>y</u>e	/ /
<u>ch</u>est	/ /		<u>v</u>ein	/ /
elbo<u>w</u>	/ /		<u>j</u>aw	/ /
stoma<u>ch</u>	/ /		<u>s</u>kin	/ /
no<u>s</u>e	/ /		<u>n</u>eck	/ /
<u>t</u>eeth	/ /		<u>th</u>umb	/ /
<u>l</u>eg	/ /		brea<u>the</u>	/ /
fi<u>n</u>ger	/ /		han<u>d</u>	/ /
<u>m</u>outh	/ /		a<u>r</u>m	/ /
<u>f</u>oot	/ /		<u>g</u>ums	/ /
<u>sh</u>oulder	/ /		vi<u>s</u>ion	/ /

What doesn't have a body but has two legs and runs?
A pair of panty hose.

Consonant Discrimination – Advanced

Use the **English Phonetic Alphabet** symbol to indicate the sound of the underlined letter in each of the words below. (Solution is on page 217.)

Ø is the symbol when the consonant is silent.

girl	/	/	sing	/	/	campaign	/	/
giant	/	/	ocean	/	/	quarter	/	/
cough	/	/	half	/	/	six	/	/
cello	/	/	antique	/	/	north	/	/
sugar	/	/	Christmas	/	/	league	/	/
usual	/	/	passion	/	/	pleasure	/	/
nation	/	/	toilet	/	/	racquet	/	/
nature	/	/	buffet	/	/	pizza	/	/
education	/	/	orange	/	/	union	/	/
question	/	/	whale	/	/	honor	/	/
answer	/	/	arctic	/	/	wished	/	/
who	/	/	please	/	/	danced	/	/
when	/	/	ache	/	/	laughed	/	/
birthday	/	/	choir	/	/	asked	/	/
sign	/	/	dogs	/	/	social	/	/
busy	/	/	cats	/	/	button	/	/
vehicle	/	/	walk	/	/	Europe	/	/
names	/	/	exit	/	/	garage	/	/
Asia	/	/	February	/	/	both	/	/
comb	/	/	century	/	/	print	/	/

What is the saddest sea mammal?
The blue whale

Terrible T – Advanced

Print the EPA symbol for the underlined Ts in the following words. The first one is done for you. (Solution is on page 218.)

Word	Symbol		Word	Symbol	
<u>t</u>ime	/ t /		posi<u>t</u>ion	/ /	
wa<u>t</u>er	/ /		<u>st</u>art	/ /,	/ /
quali<u>t</u>y	/ /		<u>st</u>ar<u>t</u>ed	/ /,	/ /
spaghe<u>tt</u>i	/ /		po<u>t</u>a<u>t</u>o	/ /,	/ /
pho<u>t</u>o	/ /		in<u>t</u>erna<u>t</u>ional	/ /,	/ /
pho<u>t</u>ography	/ /		furni<u>t</u>ure	/ /	
na<u>t</u>ure	/ /		bracele<u>t</u>	/ /	
in<u>t</u>erne<u>t</u>	/ /,	/ /	compu<u>t</u>er	/ /	
ci<u>t</u>y	/ /		a<u>t</u>trac<u>t</u>ive	/ /,	/ /
exci<u>t</u>ing	/ /		wha<u>t</u>	/ /	
lis<u>t</u>en	/ /		deb<u>t</u>	/ /	
li<u>tt</u>le	/ /		re<u>t</u>ire	/ /	
wri<u>tt</u>en	/ /		<u>T</u>uesday	/ /	
sof<u>t</u>en	/ /		whis<u>t</u>le	/ /	
<u>t</u>sunami	/ /		<u>T</u>hompson	/ /	
<u>t</u>hyme	/ /		Connec<u>t</u>icu<u>t</u>	/ /,	/ /
pi<u>zz</u>a	/ /		coun<u>t</u>er	/ /	
<u>t</u>empera<u>t</u>ure	/ /,	/ /	in<u>t</u>elligen<u>t</u>	/ /,	/ /
Chris<u>t</u>ian	/ /		con<u>t</u>ras<u>t</u>	/ /,	/ /
<u>t</u>oma<u>t</u>o	/ /,	/ /	foun<u>t</u>ain	/ /	
pho<u>t</u>ograph	/ /		Bri<u>t</u>ish	/ /	
Dako<u>t</u>a	/ /		con<u>t</u>en<u>t</u>	/ /,	/ /
mi<u>tt</u>en	/ /		capi<u>t</u>al	/ /	
moun<u>t</u>ain	/ /		as<u>th</u>ma	/ /	
uni<u>t</u>ed	/ /		sen<u>t</u>ence	/ /	

What's the laziest vegetable?
The couch potato

English is Stupid, pages 42 to 44

The Wedding of Grammar and Pronunciation

Plural S

Words for Plural S Exercise and Third-Person Singular

The next few exercises are some of my favourites because students often have familiarity with the rules of grammar for making plurals, adding **s** in the third-person singular, and the simple past. However, they have seldom thought of the *sounds* this way before. This really starts to **reprogram their brains for speaking**. Teasing apart writing from speaking is hard work. Advanced students sometimes think, **oh, this exercise is too easy for me!** Then they have trouble. Students need to learn to separate spelling from sounds.

Pronunciation Rules for S

Either for Plural or the Ridiculous S on the Third-Person Singular

1) Words ending in /f/, /k/, /p/, /t/ make the sound /s/ when **s** is added:

laugh	/laf/	laughs	cup	/kup/	cups
drink	/driNgk/	drinks	bat	/bat/	bats

2) Words ending in /j/, /s/, /z/, /ch/, /sh/, /zh/ make the sound /iz/ when **es** is added:

fridge	/frij/	fridges	bench	/bench/	benches
fox	/foks/	foxes	wish	/wish/	wishes
buzz	/buz/	buzzes	garage	/garazh/	garages

3) The rest of the endings make the sound /z/ when **s** is added:
   /b/, /d/, /g/, /l/, /m/, /n/, /r/, /w/, /y/...
   and all words ending in vowel sounds.

cab	/kab/	cabs	name	/naym/	names
head	/hed/	heads	wine	/wiyn/	wines
dog	/dog/	dogs	toe	/tow/	toes
ball	/bol/	balls	knee	/ney/	knees

S on the end of a word usually makes the sound /z/

English is Stupid, page 40

Chapter One • Grammar Connections • Consonants

What Sound Does the Final *s* Make?

This page is available in color as a free download from the resource page of www.thompsonlanguagecenter.com.

Chapter One Grammar Connections Consonants

Singular/Plural

Make the clothing words on page 61 plural and print the plural words in the column under the sound their **s** makes: /s/ as in **shirt<u>s</u>**, /z/ as in **tie<u>s</u>** or /iz/ and in **dress<u>es</u>**. (Solution is on page 218.)

/s/	/z/	/iz/
/f/, /k/, /p/, /t/	/b/, /d/, /g/, /l/, /m/, /n/, /r/, /v/, /w/, /y/…	/ch/, /j/, /s/, /z/, /Sh/, Zh/
shirts	ties	dresses

Why did the golfer wear two pairs of pants?
In case he got a hole in one.

English is Stupid, page 40

Pronunciation Rules
Simple Past Tense of Regular Verbs
(Solutions are on page 218.)

1. The regular simple past tense always ends in the letters **ed**. There are, however, three different pronunciations for the final sound of the regular simple past.

/t/	/d/	/id/
danc<u>ed</u>	call<u>ed</u>	add<u>ed</u>

2. The final sound is pronounced **/t/** after the air-out sounds **/f/, /k/, /p/, /s/, /CH/** and **/Sh/**.

cough	cough<u>ed</u>
talk	talk<u>ed</u>
shop	shopp<u>ed</u>
kiss	kiss<u>ed</u>
watch	watch<u>ed</u>
wash	wash<u>ed</u>

3. The final sound is pronounced **/d/** after sounds **/b/, /g/, /j/, /l/, /m/, /n/, /Ng/, /r/, /Th/, /v/, /z/,** and **/Zh/**.

rub	rubb<u>ed</u>
tug	tugg<u>ed</u>
charge	charg<u>ed</u>
call	call<u>ed</u>
name	nam<u>ed</u>
learn	learn<u>ed</u>
bang	bang<u>ed</u>
order	order<u>ed</u>
bathe	bath<u>ed</u>
love	lov<u>ed</u>
confuse	confus<u>ed</u>
massage	massag<u>ed</u>

4. The final sound is pronounced **/d/** after all vowel sounds.

agree	agre<u>ed</u>
play	play<u>ed</u>
glue	glu<u>ed</u>
enjoy	enjoy<u>ed</u>

5. The final sound is pronounced **/id/** after **/d/** and **/t/**. For your information (**FYI**), **/id/** adds a syllable to the verb.

start	start<u>ed</u>
decide	decid<u>ed</u>

English is Stupid, page 44

Past Tense of Regular Verbs – Basic

Read each past-tense verb out loud and place it in the correct column. The first one has been completed as an example. (Solution is on page 218.)

look	turn	wait
ask	cook	study
move	taste	state
spell	plant	dance
report	cry	shave
hand	talk	live
wish	brush	play
add	start	bake

-*ed* sounds like /t/	-*ed* sounds like /d/	-*ed* sounds like /id/
looked		

 FYI: A colourful set of 24 *Past-Tense Cards* that work perfectly with this exercise is available from the e-store at ThompsonLanguageCenter.com.

Why did the lion spit out the clown?
Because it tasted funny.

English is Stupid, page 44

Past Tense Regular Verbs – Advanced

Read each past-tense verb out loud and place into the correct column. The first one has been completed as an example. (Solution is on page 218.)

relax	exchange	litter
erase	vacuum	befriend
operate	insert	brainstorm
finish	compute	supervise
unscramble	fertilize	videotape
text	attach	request
manufacture	type	immigrate
comprehend	capitalize	laugh

-ed sounds like /t/	-ed sounds like /d/	-ed sounds like /id/
relaxed		

★ **FYI:** A colourful set of 24 *Past-Tense Cards* that work perfectly with this exercise is available from the e-store at ThompsonLanguageCenter.com. ★

 A mouse family was chased by a cat. The mother mouse turned around and barked, *Woof! Woof!* The surprised cat ran away. The mother mouse smiled and said, *You see, it pays to learn a second language!*

Mystery Word Match Series

15 Minutes of Fun

In these exercises, students simply match the description with a word in the answer box at the bottom of the page, and then print the word in the space provided.

These exercises are versatile and fun for every student level, great as add-ons and 15-minute fillers. Have one of these exercises sitting on the students' desks as they trickle into class as a warm-up (the early birds have something to do, and the late ones get value when the exercise is taken up). **Mystery Word Match** works great when there is 15 minutes to fill before break or at the end of the day. These exercises are great for a review, warm-ups, vocabulary building, and friendly competition.

This style of exercise is easy to customize for your class. There is a wide array of topics and sounds featured. For the lowest levels, study the vocabulary beforehand and give the exercise to the students in groups. Higher-level beginners may work in pairs. To make the same exercise more difficult for intermediate students, cover the answer box at the bottom of the page when photocopying. Depending on the class, students may work in groups, pairs or on their own, and with the answers available or not.

(Some teachers do well making racing games out of these, but not me. I feel that a race always makes someone a loser.)

There are mixed levels of difficulty, and these are indicated at the top of each page. There are extra exercises that focus on sounds for some language groups, tricky consonant blends and difficult sounds.

Basic: The designated sound occurs at the **beginning** of the answer word.

Advanced: The designated sound occurs **somewhere** in the word. The vocabulary and explanations are more difficult.

The solutions for this Mystery Match series begin on page 219.

Words that Start with /b/ – Basic

What words starting with /b/ answers the statements below?

1.	Hair growing on a man's chin, rhymes with weird	
2.	A male that has the same parents as another member of the family	
3.	Cows have calves, horses have foals, dogs have puppies, and people have …	
4.	Clay shaped into blocks and baked until they are hard enough to make houses.	
5.	Room with a sink and a toilet is a two-piece; add a bath and shower, and it's a four-piece	
6.	Action word for money spent at the store for shopping; purchase	
7.	This usually starts the answer to a **why** question.	
8.	Federal institution where people save or borrow money	
9.	Canoe, yacht, ship and barge are all different kinds	
10.	Lengths of hard, white calcium that make up the skeleton; a picture of them is an x-ray.	
11.	Summer, strawberry or bleached – it is the color of Marilyn Monroe's hair.	
12.	Big piece of furniture with a mattress that is used for sleeping	
13.	Two-wheeled vehicle for transportation or recreation	
14.	Red root vegetable that stains – it is good boiled or pickled.	

because	beet	blond	bed
bones	brother	babies	bricks
bank	buy	boat	bicycle
bathroom	beard		

Chapter One — Mystery Match — Consonants

Words that Start with /d/ – Basic

What words starting with **/d/** answers the statements below?

1.	Entrance to a house or a room swings opens and closed	
2.	Long and formal as a gown or short and light for summer – only women wear this type of clothing.	
3.	Mother is to Father, as Mommy is to Daddy, as Mom is to ___	
4.	Deep-fried circle of dough iced with sugar or chocolate and eaten with a cup of coffee	
5.	Animal that quacks and can fly in the air, swim in the water and walk on the land	
6.	A hole in the bottom of the sink or bathtub that lets the water out	
7.	Tooth-care professional who recommends brushing and flossing twice a day	
8.	Almighty unit of money in Canada and the USA	
9.	Covered in brown bits of soil after working or playing in the garden	
10.	Classrooms are filled with rows of these where students sit and study	
11.	*Man's best friend*, this popular pet is more faithful and obedient than a cat.	
12.	Use a pencil or crayon to make a picture on a piece of paper	
13.	Irregular past-tense form of drink; rhymes with *thank*	
14.	Chemicals used to change the color of cloth or hair	

doughnut	dye	door	dollar
dentist	Dad	dress	drank
drain	dirty	dog	desks
duck	draw		

© Judy Thompson 2011

Chapter One — Mystery Match — Consonants

Words that Start with /g/ – Basic

What words starting with **/g/** answers the statements below?

1.	Separate places for four separate fingers and a thumb in this piece of cloth to keep a hand warm	
2.	Small round purple or green fruit that grows in bunches	
3.	Superlative is **best**, comparative is **better** – what is the adjective?	
4.	The color of pickles, grass and the traffic light that means **go**	
5.	Where *Mary, Mary, quite contrary* and everyone else's flowers grow	
6.	Halloween is a special night for these spooky spirits.	
7.	Monopoly, Scrabble, soccer, football and tag – what children like to play	
8.	Set of sentence rules especially important for ESL students learning to write	
9.	Tiny, silly little laugh that rhymes with wiggle	
10.	Popular outdoor activity developed in Scotland with 18 holes, tees, fairways and sand-traps	
11.	Fuel for cars that is being slowly replaced by renewable energy sources	
12.	*God be with you* has been shortened over the years to this common phrase when someone leaves.	
13.	To understand a joke and laugh is to _ _ _ it.	
14.	Weekly kitchen and household goods people buy at the food store	

glove	games	golf	green
garden	grapes	grammar	good
giggle	get	good-bye	ghosts
gas	groceries		

© Judy Thompson 2011 — www.ThompsonLanguageCenter.com

Chapter One Mystery Match Consonants

Words that Start with /h/ – basic

What words starting with /h/ answers the statements below?

1.	What kind of birthday are you going to have?	
2.	*Wh* question asking for a person's name	
3.	Four fingers, a thumb and a palm at the end of each arm	
4.	Subject pronoun for male third-person singular	
5.	When something weighs so much, it can't easily be picked up.	
6.	It is the *North American dream* that everyone own their own place to live.	
7.	Everyone likes to give it, but no one likes to ask for it – but we all need it sometimes.	
8.	Brown, black, blond, gray or red, it's the stuff that grows on peoples' heads.	
9.	More and more people are exercising and eating well because they want to take care of their _ _ _ _ _ _ .	
10.	To laugh at jokes and see *the lighter side of* life – we all need a sense of this.	
11.	Fast food that people in #9 don't eat – a wiener in a bun with mustard, ketchup and relish	
12.	Drive fast on these multi-lane super roads that crisscross the nation	
13.	A school subject that studies events of the past	
14.	Feeling in the stomach that drives people to the kitchen to get something to eat	

highways	health	heavy	help
hand	humor	he	who
hunger	hair	history	happy
hotdog	house		

Chapter One — Mystery Match — Consonants

Words with /j/ in them – Advanced

What words with the sound /j/ in them answers the statements below?

1.	The most popular month for weddings; summer holidays start here	
2.	Soft, chewy, fruit-flavoured gumdrops	
3.	Weights, dumbbells, stationary bikes, treadmills and trainers help people keep fit here.	
4.	Jolly green fellow of frozen vegetable fame	
5.	Institutions of higher learning are formal places to acquire one of these.	
6.	Too much traffic or a sweet fruit spread for toast	
7.	Sweet, creamy, butter-rich candy with flavours like chocolate, maple, orange swirl and turtle	
8.	When you need information, ask a _ _ _ _ _ _ _ _.	
9.	Army, navy, air force and marines are groups of these professional warriors.	
10.	Affecting almost everyone, or a non-specific quantity, or the highest ranking officer	
11.	A bit of fun told at parties or in the school yard just to make people laugh	
12.	Special sets of words and expressions unique to a workplace or field of study	
13.	The first name of Queen Elizabeth's father; _ _ _ _ _ _ Bush; an old-fashioned man's name	
14.	The part of a machine that produces the power	

joke	engine	fudge	general
June	question	jargon	gym
giant	jam	jujubes	education
George	soldiers		

Chapter One — Mystery Match — Consonants

Words that Start with /kw/ – Basic

What words starting with **/kw/** answers the statements below?

1.	Bee that rules the hive; Kate when William is king	
2.	Organized group of singers that practice together and perform weekly at church services	
3.	What people want when they say *Shhh!*	
4.	Twenty-five cent piece named for its fraction of a dollar	
5.	Hard glassy white rock used for making clocks and watches accurate	
6.	An outdated description of a verbal disagreement between people that leads to a falling out	
7.	Warm patchwork cover for a bed that is sewn from scrap pieces of fabric and stuffed with batting	
8.	Teachers can surprise their students with one of these short tests	
9.	A French province in Canada with a capital city by the same name	
10.	Abrupt finish to a job or task before the work has ended	
11.	Typing training sentence that uses every letter on the keyboard, *The _ _ _ _ _ brown fox jumped over the lazy dog.*	
12.	The very best value of a product or service	
13.	Nauseous feeling in the stomach from nerves, illness or bad food	
14.	Richter scale measures this shaking of the Earth	

quarrel	quake	quiet	Quebec
quit	queen	quarter	quartz
quick	quiz	quilt	choir
quality	queasy		

© Judy Thompson 2011

Words that Start with /m/ – Basic

What starting word with **/m/** answers the statements below?

1.	There are sixty of these time units in one hour.	
2.	Floor cleaning tool that is used with water, soap and a bucket	
3.	*Nature's perfect food*, white liquid from cows or cocoanuts that people drink	
4.	A mega-building with many stores where teenagers hangout, meet their friends and buy clothes	
5.	Water, honeydew and cantaloupe are varieties of this juicy fruit.	
6.	*Dirty yellow* as a color and delicious on hotdogs as a condiment	
7.	The doctor gives prescriptions for pills or tonic to buy at the pharmacy when people are sick.	
8.	First day of the work week	
9.	Fingers together and thumbs apart in this warm winter hand protection	
10.	April showers bring flowers in the next month	
11.	Made from corn, canola or sunflower oil, this vegetable product is a substitute for butter.	
12.	*The dawn's early light* is the description in the American national anthem for a time of day.	
13.	Professional car maintenance and repair occupation	
14.	*Oral* is the Latin word that refers to this talking and chewing part of the face	

mustard	mitten	margarine	mouth
milk	mop	melon	May
mechanic	morning	Monday	medicine
minutes	mall		

Chapter One — Mystery Match — Consonants

Words that Start with /n/ – Basic

What words starting with /n/ answers the statements below?

1.	Brother or sister's son, the male form of niece	
2.	Time of the day when the sun is at its highest point and lunch is served	
3.	Sharp utensils at the right-hand side of a place setting, used for cutting food	
4.	A person, place or thing in English grammar; common ones don't have a capital, but proper ones do	
5.	Flexible joints that connect the bones of the fingers and the fingers to the hands	
6.	A long, thin, sharp sliver of steel with a tiny eye used for sewing clothes	
7.	A part of the body between the head and shoulders	
8.	Developed in Greece in 2,000 BC, they are the symbols used for mathematics.	
9.	Information about what is happening in the world every day	
10.	Long, cold, dark and miserable, it's the eleventh month of the year.	
11.	Traditionally, women were trained to give needles and help doctors; now men often practice this occupation as well.	
12.	Part of the face that sniffs and runs when it is cold	
13.	A bad chest cold can develop into this serious infection with fluid in the lungs	
14.	Big joint halfway down the leg that lets humans walk and sit on the couch	

knuckles	needle	numbers	pneumonia
nurse	noon	knives	November
knee	nose	noun	nephew
news	neck		

© Judy Thompson 2011 — www.ThompsonLanguageCenter.com

Words that Start with /p/ – Basic

What word starting with **/p/** answers the statements below?

1.	Make music with a piano, have fun, or take part in a game	
2.	Someone with good manners asks for things using this *magic word.*	
3.	Section of a whole or a role in a theatrical production	
4.	Say English individual words exactly as native English speakers say them	
5.	Set the table with knives, forks, spoons and these flat dishes that people eat from	
6.	The round underground vegetable in *chips;* also served mashed, baked and French fried	
7.	Baby cats are kittens; baby chickens are chicks; what is a baby dog?	
8.	Gifts usually wrapped with ribbon and colored paper, then topped with a bow	
9.	Ink-filled instrument used to write, mostly on paper	
10.	This activity *makes perfect;* ESL learners do it every day to improve their English.	
11.	Irregular past tense form of pay; it rhymes with *made.*	
12.	A game made from a picture on cardboard, cut into many notched pieces to be fit back together	
13.	Large, juicy tropical fruit with brown pointy skin	
14.	Lilacs, eggplant and grapes; mix the primary colors blue and red to paint in this color.	

please	paid	part	purple
practice	play	pineapple	pen
puppy	plates	presents	puzzle
potato	pronounce		

Chapter One — Mystery Match — Consonants

Words that Start with /r/ – Basic

What word starting with /r/ answers the statements below?

1.	Flexible joint that connects the arm to the hand	
2.	Large, privately owned tract of land; home for the cowboy and his livestock or a creamy salad dressing	
3.	Brides wear them on their left hand and the planet Saturn wears them, too.	
4.	Large African animal with tough skin and a big pointed horn on its nose	
5.	Root vegetable that is red on the outside and white on the inside; it adds color to garden salads.	
6.	The opposite of *right*, not the opposite of *write* or *left*	
7.	Mother Goose is a collection of children's nursery _ _ _ _ _ _ that are useful for ESL students to study.	
8.	Cat-sized wild animal has a mask like a bandit and a ringed tail. He has adapted too well to city life and is a pest.	
9.	Sweet/tangy red fruit from a prickly bush makes fantastic pies and tarts.	
10.	Strong cord made from natural fibres like hemp or synthetic fibres like nylon	
11.	Garden tool with metal fingers for gathering leaves and cut grass in the yard	
12.	A circular Christmas decoration made from bows and greenery and hung on the front door	
13.	Grain for making *light* or *dark* deli loaves of bread	
14.	Gear for going backwards in a motor vehicle	

wreath	reverse	wrist	rake
rings	rope	rhymes	raspberries
wrong	ranch	raccoon	rhino
radish	rye		

© Judy Thompson 2011

Words that Start with /v/ – Basic

What word starting with /v/ answers the statements below?

1.	Word or group of words that convey an *action* in English grammar	
2.	Edible plants grown in gardens sold in the produce section of the grocery store	
3.	Special doctor who treats sick and injured animals	
4.	The right and responsibility to participate in an election	
5.	Lines running from side to side are horizontal; what are lines running up and down?	
6.	Grapes and roses grow on these plants that like to climb up on trellises and houses.	
7.	Official government permit to live or work in another country **or** a credit card.	
8.	Poetry – lines written with a regular rhythm, and the ends of the lines rhyme	
9.	The Roman goddess of love and beauty, or the second planet from the sun	
10.	A family vehicle that is larger than a car, closed in and carries more people than a truck	
11.	Human sound used to talk or sing; with a bad sore throat, it can be lost.	
12.	Person who casually drops in or is formally invited to spend time at another's house	
13.	Work without pay for a charity or to gain experience in a professional field	
14.	There are more than one million in this group of words that makes up the English language.	

veterinarian	voice	Venus	vote
van	vertical	visa	vines
verse	vegetables	verb	visitor
volunteer	vocabulary		

Chapter One — Mystery Match — Consonants

Words that Start with /w/ – Basic

What word starting with **/w/** answers the statements below?

1.	The irregular past tense of go; rhymes with *rent*	
2.	Glass rectangles that let light into buildings, or a Microsoft program	
3.	First numeral; where counting starts; the only	
4.	Above the hips and below the chest, it should be the narrowest part of the torso	
5.	This color represents purity and is often worn by western brides.	
6.	Known as *hump day,* this day falls in the middle of the work week.	
7.	The answer to this *Wh* question is a place.	
8.	Hired to exert mental and physical energy in order to earn money	
9.	Niagara has a globally recognized magnificent example of this geographical marvel.	
10.	The owl is an animal symbol that represents the accumulation of knowledge.	
11.	Bicycles have two, cars have four, and semis have eighteen.	
12.	An event that happened a single time and was not repeated.	
13.	Made from animal fat, oils or paraffin, it burns slowly and works well shaped into candles	
14.	Put one foot in front of the other; go somewhere by foot.	

waist	walk	where	one
Wednesday	worker	wax	went
wheels	once	white	windows
wise	waterfall		

© Judy Thompson 2011

Words that Start with /y/ – Basic

What word with /y/ answers the statements below?

1.	The sunny color of daffodils, lemons and bananas	
2.	Creamy milk product with fruit and probiotics added for flavour and health	
3.	Spain, Portugal, France, Germany and Italy are a few of the counties in this Atlantic continent.	
4.	365¼ days, fifty-two weeks or a twelve-month period	
5.	Expensive post-secondary institution for degrees and professional school	
6.	Wool from sheep is clipped, cleaned, spun and dyed into this thick thread for knitting clothing.	
7.	The twenty-first letter of the Latin alphabet, the fifth vowel	
8.	A famous Beatles' song; the day before today	
9.	Bright orange cousin of the potato, it is considered a *super food*.	
10.	Pilots, police officers, soldiers and doormen wear one of these to work.	
11.	A father sheep is a ram, a baby sheep is a lamb – what is a mother sheep?	
12.	Set of exercises to relax the mind and body	
13.	Agree, give permission and understand – all in one little affirmative word	
14.	Beautiful, mythical horse with a single spiral horn from its forehead	

yes	unicorn	yarn	Europe
uniform	yesterday	u	yoga
yogurt	university	yellow	year
ewe	yam		

Chapter One — Mystery Match — Consonants

Words with /z/ in them – Advanced

What word starting with /z/ answers the statements below?

1.	Sharp tool used to cut material such as paper or hair	
2.	Black and white striped African animal that is related to the horse	
3.	A possessive pronoun that indicates something belongs to a female	
4.	Length, height, weight, area or volume measurements	
5.	A fastener, a ribbon of tiny metal teeth that lock together to close a coat or pair of jeans	
6.	Critical set of academic tests at the end of the school year	
7.	_ _ _ _ _ _ are red and violets are blue, Sugar is sweet and so are you.	
8.	Physically or metaphorically grab something with a sudden and strong grip	
9.	To claim another person's ideas as one's own	
10.	Demonstrate how an exercise is to be completed by providing a model	
11.	Identify something as familiar; seen or heard before	
12.	An adjective to describe something that is not difficult	
13.	Physical activity done to maintain or improve one's health	
14.	All garments worn by anyone – men, women, or children	

hers	zipper	clothes	exercise
scissors	recognize	size	exams
easy	roses	example	seize
zebra	plagiarize		

© Judy Thompson 2011 — www.ThompsonLanguageCenter.com

Words with /ch/ in them – Advanced

What word with /ch/ answers the statements below?

1.	With four legs and a back, it is not a living thing but somewhere to sit.	
2.	Ticking timepiece worn on the wrist and never needs winding	
3.	Books are divided into these numbered sections.	
4.	Roof structure that allows smoke and furnace fumes to escape from the house.	
5.	Small strong specialty coffee from Italy	
6.	Forest, rivers, mountains, animals and birds – wild and untouched by man	
7.	Color that is dark, dark gray, almost black; or as briquettes, it is chunks of fuel for an old-fashioned barbecue.	
8.	Monetary units, smaller than bills carried loose in pockets or purse compartments	
9.	Paintings or digital memories framed and hung as decorations on the wall	
10.	Baby birds emerge from their shells this way.	
11.	In the string section of the orchestra, it looks like a large violin.	
12.	Solid, creamy, sliceable dairy product produced in almost every culture.	
13.	Hospitals use x-ray machines to detect this break in a bone.	
14.	Artistic creations carved from stone or welded in metal	

sculpture	watch	nature	cheese
charcoal	pictures	hatch	change
cello	cappuccino	chimney	chapter
fracture	chair		

Chapter One — Mystery Match — Consonants

Words that Start with /sh/ – Basic

What word starting with **/sh/** answers the statements below?

1.	The opposite of out-going; people sometimes feel this way meeting strangers.	
2.	Word used to give advice, opinions or probability	
3.	Natural sweetener for coffee and tea; one lump or two?	
4.	Fleece is the coat that is shorn from these woolly farm animals. Baa baa black _ _ _ _ _, have you any wool?	
5.	Certainty, absolute confidence in the information	
6.	He wears a white apron, a tall white hat, and cooks in a fancy restaurant.	
7.	Popular daily hygiene that uses less water and time than a bath.	
8.	The sun, a new car and a big smile all do this brightly.	
9.	Geometric figures that include squares, circles, triangles and rectangles, etc.	
10.	When a man takes a razor to his chin and a woman takes one to her legs, what are they doing?	
11.	Subject pronoun: the female form of *he*	
12.	Going to the mall to purchase food, clothes or house wares	
13.	Expensive bubbly alcoholic drink *cracked open* for very special occasions	
14.	Liquid soap made especially for washing hair	

sure	should	chef	shine
shaving	shopping	sugar	she
champagne	sheep	shapes	shy
shampoo	shower		

© Judy Thompson 2011 — www.ThompsonLanguageCenter.com

Words that Start with /TH/ – Basic

What word with **/TH/** answers the statements below?

1.	The day after Wednesday, named after the god of thunder	
2.	Working outside on a hot summer day makes you feel like you want a drink.	
3.	Show appreciation and good manners with this magic two-word phrase.	
4.	Rhymes with *pink;* it is what the brain is supposed to do.	
5.	Glass instrument with a thin tube of mercury that measures temperature	
6.	The top part of a leg, one of the dark meat portions of a cooked chicken	
7.	Irregular past-tense form of the verb throw	
8.	Divide a pie into three equal parts to make this fraction	
9.	Someone who takes or steals things that don't belong to them.	
10.	Fine cotton string that comes on a spool; loop the end through a needle in order to sew	
11.	When people don't weight enough, it can be unhealthy; they are too _ _ _ _	
12.	This purple prickle bush is the emblem of Scotland.	
13.	The answer to four times eight plus one is a hard number to say.	
14.	Four fingers and one of these on each hand	

think	thirsty	thistle	thief
thread	Thursday	threw	third
thirty-three	thumb	thank you	thin
thigh	thermometer		

Words with /Ng/ in them – Advanced

What word with /Ng/ answers the statements below?

1.	Three-sided, two-dimensional geometric shape	
2.	Prince William will one day hold this title in Great Britain.	
3.	Light red makes a new hue, the color of bubble gum	
4.	Only one; the status of an adult who is not in a romantic relationship	
5.	Crazy language spoken by more than 1.5 billion people around the world	
6.	There's one in the kitchen and one in the bathroom for washing food and hands	
7.	With greater muscle mass, men are physically able to lift and move heavy things; they are …	
8.	Carefully measured, hammered a nail into the wall and mounted a picture	
9.	Big orange primates popular in zoos because they behave so much like humans.	
10.	Oral mode of communication that changes totally across civilizations.	
11.	Don't do this before driving a car.	
12.	Relative measure of distance or time for example; Australia is a _ _ _ _ way away or a century is a _ _ _ _ time.	
13.	Present continuous verb form or gerund that means vocalizing musically	
14.	This pesky, stinky rodent is black with a white stripe down its back and is the size of a house cat.	

skunk	singing	strong	pink
orangutan	sink	triangle	hung
single	king	language	English
long	drink		

Words with /zh/ in them – Advanced

What word with **/zh/** answers the statements below?

1.	Structure beside the house for parking, fixing or storing automobiles	
2.	Off white; the light tan color of a sandy beach or a coffee with double cream	
3.	Flat screen, LED or old fashioned tube-style home entertainment unit	
4.	Normal or common behaviour or activity	
5.	India's most famous landmark; the headstone for a beloved wife	
6.	The color of the tropical waters of the Caribbean Sea	
7.	"I was delighted to do that for you. It was my absolute _____."	
8.	Originally from France, it's the powder make-up that is applied to cheeks to give the appearance of blushing.	
9.	Relaxing therapeutic treatment where someone else rubs your muscles	
10.	The desert can play tricks on a traveler's eyes, and they can see things that aren't there.	
11.	The only word in English that begins with the sound /Zh/. It means type or category.	
12.	A natural remedy to prevent or minimize the symptoms of the common cold	
13.	Worn on the wrist or the front of the gown, the boy buys this custom-created flower arrangement for his prom date.	
14.	The largest continent on Earth – home to the greatest number of people	

corsage	azure	mirage	rouge
garage	massage	pleasure	usual
Taj Mahal	beige	Asia	Echinacea
television	genre		

Consonant Sound Maze

Instructions

Enter the maze at the ⬇ in the top left corner.

Connect the words that <u>start with</u> (Basic) or <u>contain</u> (Advanced) the sound indicated in the title of the worksheet, i.e., /b/.

Do not lift your pen from the page.

Do not cross over a solid line – only go through gaps in the lines on the sides, top or bottom of the word square.

Exit the maze at the ⬇ using the shortest route possible.

Teacher note: For lower levels, stick to the Basic series and have the students complete the exercise in a group. It is helpful if they read the words out loud to each other.

(Solutions to the consonant sound mazes begin on page 220.)

 **Pet Peeves**

A dad went into a pet store and asked if he could have a cat for his son. The owner said: *Sorry, we don't do trades.*

What is more amazing than a talking dog?
                 A spelling bee

How did the dog stop the DVD player?
             He pressed the paws button.

What dog keeps the best time?
                   A watchdog

Chapter One — Sound Maze — Consonants

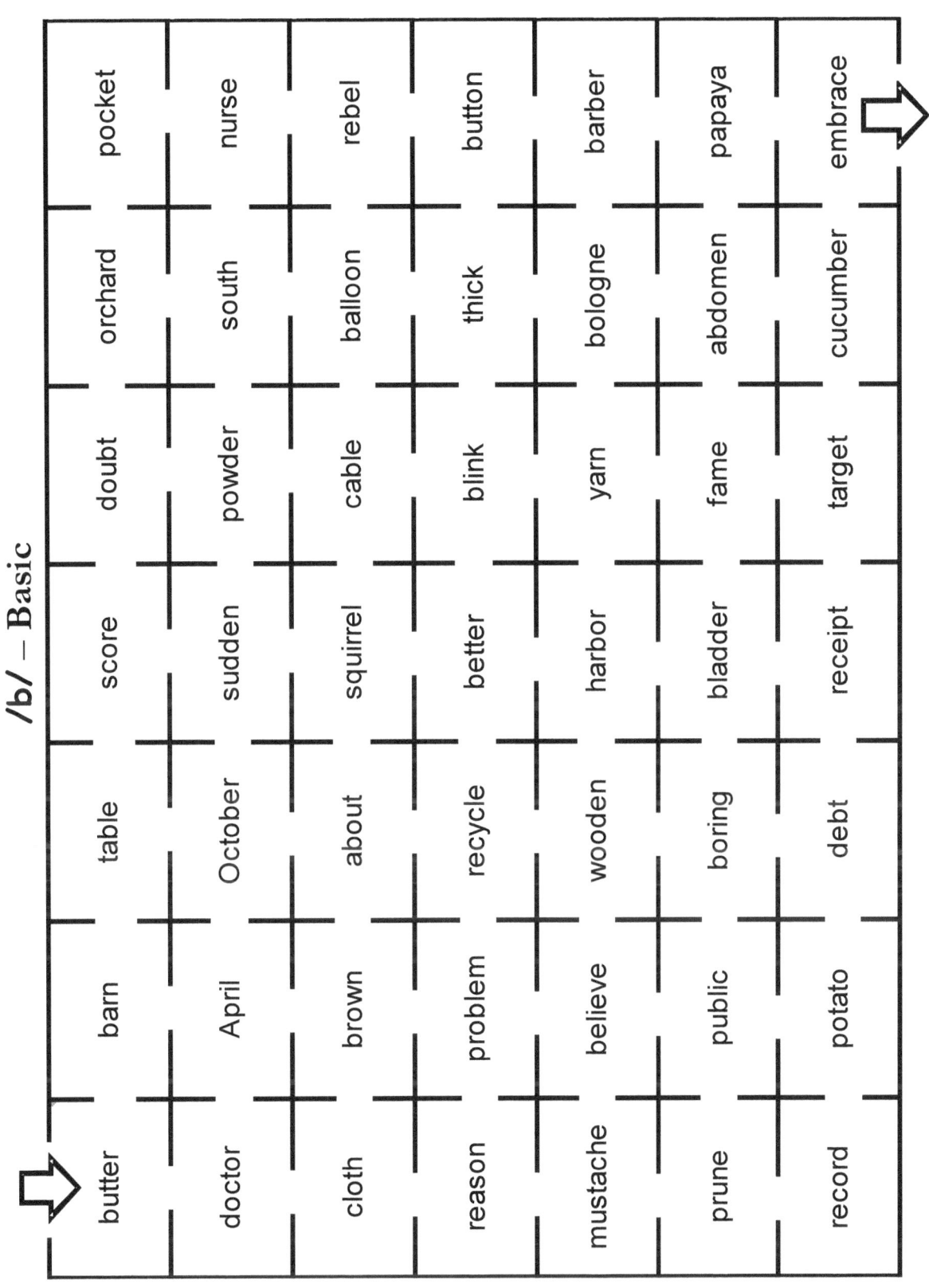

/b/ – Basic

butter	barn	table	score	doubt	orchard	pocket
doctor	April	October	sudden	powder	south	nurse
cloth	brown	about	squirrel	cable	balloon	rebel
reason	problem	recycle	better	blink	thick	button
mustache	believe	wooden	harbor	yarn	bologne	barber
prune	public	boring	bladder	fame	abdomen	papaya
record	potato	debt	receipt	target	cucumber	embrace

Chapter One — Sound Maze — Consonants

/d/ — Spelled with t or tt

→ water	pretty	goose	hundred	wheel	turnip	worm
insect	potato	machine	sixteen	thirsty	computer	butter
reported	arctic	jelly	secretary	lettuce	squash	Saturday
forty	normal	monkey	turtle	yesterday	night	fifty
little	photograph	raccoon	poetic	peaches	daughter	political
receipt	automatic	hospital	system	salon	justice	apartment
position	shampoo	tenant	necklace	grocery	society	spaghetti →

© Judy Thompson 2011 — www.ThompsonLanguageCenter.com

Chapter One Sound Maze Consonants

/f/ – Advanced
Spellings: ph, gh

though	ghost	eight	path	truth	theater	phat →
trough	graph	physician	symphony	scratch	doubt	physio
nephew	daughter	straight	cough	through	dough	tough
physics	trophy	length	phonetic	photo	bough	phase
thought	enough	night	stitch	laughter	rough	paragraph
pharmacy	laugh	general	bar-b-que	neighbor	expect	change
→ phone	plough	either	stripes	casual	watches	escape

© Judy Thompson 2011   www.ThompsonLanguageCenter.com

/k/ – Advanced
Spellings: k, c, ch, x, q

kettle	globe	office	bridge	hungry	ticket	frequent
cloth	chair	triangle	phone	center	heaven	harbor
quick	stomach	people	fax	column	explain	change
face	box	vanilla	tickle	machine	quiche	simple
basket	school	eraser	chocolate	growth	chemical	cucumber
cocoa	city	coffee	barbecue	impulse	winter	access
exchange	square	broccoli	scissors	jewelry	degree	monkey

→ start at "kettle", exit at "monkey"

Chapter One — Sound Maze — Consonants

/l/ – Basic

lemon →	bath	lime	street	goal	yellow	length
lake	call	care	moment	letter	cart	hotel
auto	purple	sorry	different	willow	going	linen
lung	flower	tape	clap	plate	sick	kettle
ladder	amuse	great	until	woman	polish	outlet
temple	left	hand	list	zipper	light	action
curve	whale	fill	lottery	swim	world	welcome →

Chapter One — Sound Maze — Consonants

Words that Start with /m/ – Basic

→ start at **money**; exit at **moon** →

money	wheat	here	sound	listen	plum	watch
mother	Friday	world	help	said	figure	notice
March	from	does	spell	memory	mango	million
men	mouth	mittens	animal	mist	frame	muffin
number	small	market	page	music	kidney	meat
public	loose	month	time	moblie	differ	match
high	found	mustard	merry	milk	began	moon

Words that Start with /n/ – Basic

nine	father	church	note	neck	need	feed
never	knee	game	know	king	knot	hotel
open	net	beads	nurse	print	nephew	silver
space	nice	knock	noun	sheep	nerve	quartz
touch	aunt	yoghurt	zipper	knuckle	needle	cousin
couch	build	write	years	north	fire	wife
bank	drawer	circus	bike	knife	night	nothing

Start: → nine
End: nothing →

Chapter One — Sound Maze — Consonants

/r/

plaid	home	camera	rabbit	wreath	oven	short →
February	thought	radish	paint	protest	effect	rooster
what	turn	author	depend	church	fuel	river
angry	carpet	know	quartz	drought	depth	bird
birth	quite	bent	worth	money	serve	smart
carrot	night	owl	unicorn	noise	regular	fuse
→ ribbon	which	town	trouble	address	wrist	equal

Chapter One — Sound Maze — Consonants

/Th/ – Basic +

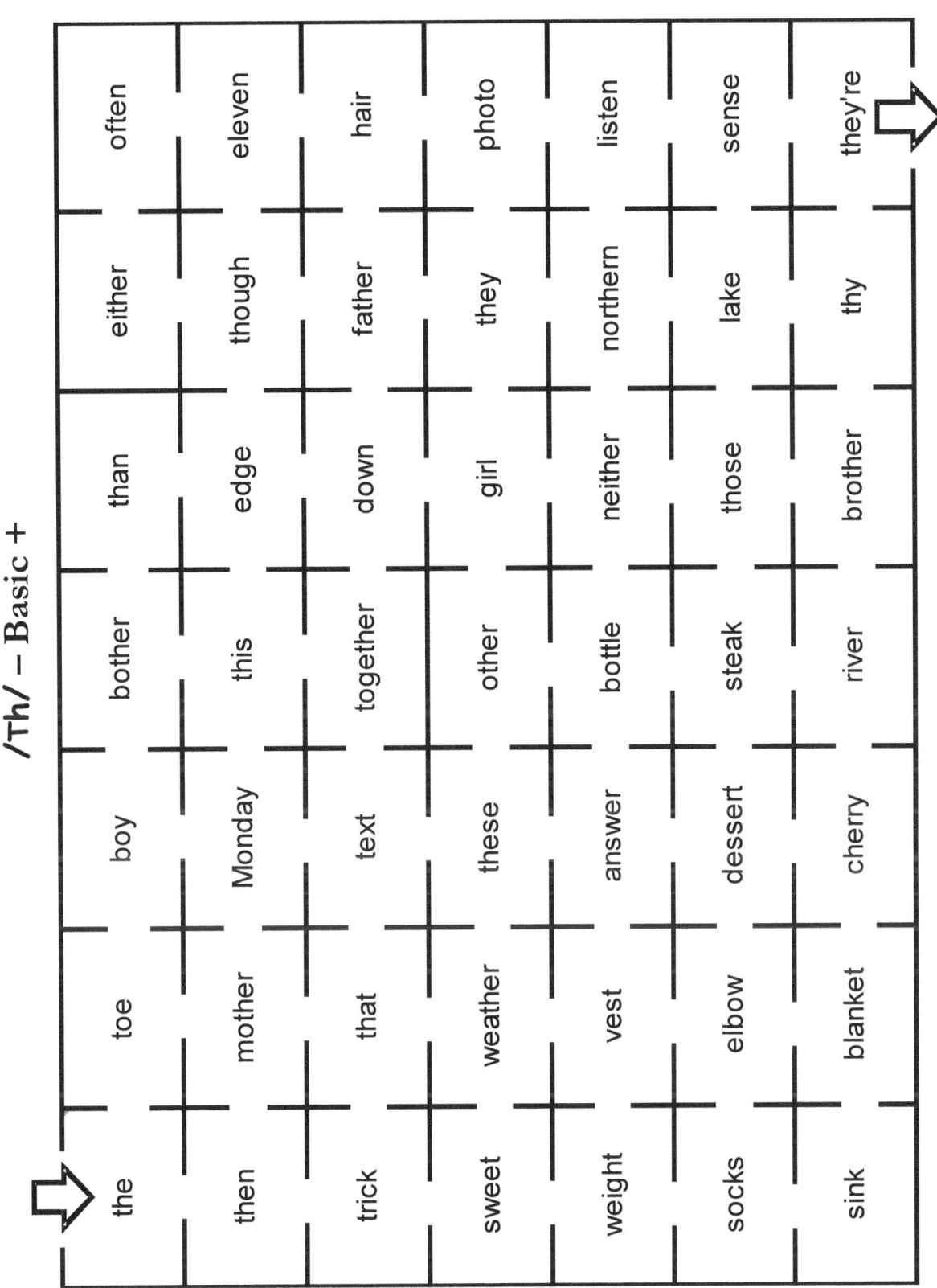

the	then	trick	sweet	weight	socks	sink
toe	mother	that	weather	vest	elbow	blanket
boy	Monday	text	these	answer	dessert	cherry
bother	this	together	other	bottle	steak	river
than	edge	down	girl	neither	those	brother
either	though	father	they	northern	lake	thy
often	eleven	hair	photo	listen	sense	they're →

The *Silent Consonants* Riddle – Basic

What letters do not make a sound in these words? (Solution is on page 221.)

write _____	Wednesday _____	clothes _____
half _____	two _____	scissors _____
knife _____	know _____	though _____
answer _____	school _____	when _____
walk _____	plumber _____	sign _____
listen _____	what _____	science _____
thumb _____	right _____	government _____
receipt _____	debt _____	autumn _____
hour _____	island _____	psychology _____
ache _____	February _____	asthma _____

Crazy English Spelling

Teacher: How do you spell 'first'?
Student: a,b,c,d,e,f,g,h,i,j,k,l,m,n,o,p,q,r,s,t,u,v,w,x,y,z
Teacher: You didn't spell first; you just recited the whole alphabet!
Student: Oh **f i r s t** is there, and the rest are silent.

English is Stupid, page 74

The *H* Riddle – Advanced

What sound does the underlined *h* make in these words? (Solution is on page 221.)

ghost _____	spaghetti _____	hors d'oeuvres _____
Christ _____	Thames _____	thyme _____
mechanic _____	character _____	rhinoceros _____
yacht _____	stomach _____	caught _____
what _____	through _____	sleigh _____
chronic _____	plough _____	zucchini _____
wheel _____	nightie _____	rhythm _____
light _____	scheme _____	chiropractor _____
Thailand _____	shepherd _____	heir _____
white _____	exhaust _____	Thompson _____
sigh _____	ghetto _____	rhyme _____
Buddha _____	taught _____	chaos _____
honest _____	where _____	vehicle _____

 What did the grape say when the elephant stepped on it?
Nothing, it just let out a little whine.

Invisible Consonants

Everyone knows about **Silent Consonants** in English – the **w** in **write** and the **k** in **knee**. The consonants are printed but don't make any sound. **Invisible Consonants** are the opposite, consonant sounds that are clearly pronounced but not represented by any letter. I can't show you a picture, because they are invisible.☺

What sound is clearly pronounced in the following words, where no letter is printed? Hint – the location of the unprinted sound is underlined. (Solution is on page 221.)

unicorn	___	beautiful	___
poet	___	pancake	___
lion	___	fluid	___
one	___	few	___
quiet	___	once	___
think	___	unit	___
fuel	___	piano	___
Europe	___	cute	___
iron	___	poem	___
cucumber	___	tire	___
uniform	___	something	___
koala	___	Cuba	___
higher	___	idea	___

Nurse: **Doctor there is a ghost in your waiting room.**
Doctor: **Tell him I can't see him.**

English is Stupid, page 74

Bingo Rules

Students love to play Bingo. Keep a jar of dry popcorn or colored plastic disks on hand as place markers for instant learning fun.

For your own classroom edition of **ESL Telephone Bingo**, photocopy both the *word list* and the *bingo card sheets* on one side only. (A very good idea is to enlarge and laminate the Bingo cards). Cut out the words on the *word list* and drop them into a dark-sided container for the caller to draw. When your class is playing, sketch the four winning Bingo patterns (shown below) on the board for their easy reference

Instructions for the students:

1. Listen for the first letter as the caller calls out a word, so when you hear **shoe**, remember the symbol /**sh**/.

2. Look to see if you have /**sh**/ on your Bingo card.

3. Place a marker over the /**sh**/ if you have it.

4. Listen for the *first letter* as the caller continues to call words.

5. Place markers over the letters that appear on your card.

6. Yell out **BINGO**! as soon as you cover the letters in a winning pattern – a straight line going **horizontally, vertically, diagonally,** or one marker in **each corner**.

Good Bingos

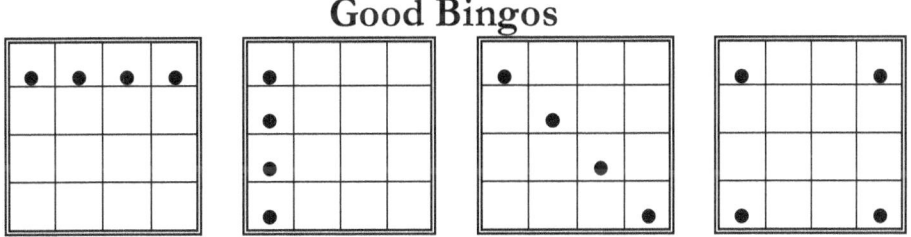

7. Call out the words corresponding to the letters you've marked in your winning pattern.

Congratulations!

The winner then becomes the caller for the next round.

Basic Consonant Bingo Word List
Game 1

book	city
doll	teach
funny	village
girl	work
home	year
jump	zoo
key	shoe
list	chest
mother	thanks
nine	the
paper	genre
rain	singing

What three keys don't open doors?
Donkey, monkey, turkey

Tricky Consonant Bingo Word List
Game 2

bridge	sandwich
drink	turtle
phone	village
ghost	window
heat	yarn
gentleman	zipper
cloud	sugar
laughter	cheese
mister	think
knee	they
puddle	Asia
write	England

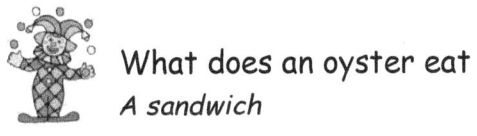

What does an oyster eat for lunch?
A sandwich

Chapter One Consonant Sounds Bingo Consonants

Card 1

/h/	/w/	/k/	/s/
/d/	/Zh/	/b/	/l/
/Sh/	/Th/	/f/	/t/
/j/	/m/	/Ch/	/p/

Card 2

/g/	/Th/	/TH/	/v/
/b/	/z/	/l/	/j/
/u/	/n/	/y/	/k/
/d/	/Ng/	/Ch/	/w/

Card 3

/w/	/h/	/b/	/Zh/
/r/	/m/	/sh/	/t/
/z/	/Ch/	/g/	/s/
/y/	/l/	/v/	/Th/

Card 4

/Zh/	/Sh/	/f/	/p/
/j/	/s/	/k/	/n/
/f/	/TH/	/m/	/Th/
/d/	/g/	/Ng/	/b/

 What's faster, heat or cold?
Heat, because you can catch a cold.

Chapter One Consonant Sounds Bingo Consonants

Card 5

/z/	/l/	/y/	/TH/
/d/	/w/	/k/	/v/
/Sh/	/p/	/r/	/g/
/f/	/t/	/Ng/	/h/

Card 6

/t/	/m/	/p/	/j/
/l/	/h/	/CH/	/Th/
/y/	/r/	/Zh/	/h/
/s/	/k/	/b/	/w/

Card 7

/w/	/Sh/	/v/	/r/
/t/	/h/	/Th/	/z/
/TH/	/p/	/y/	/l/
/s/	/Ng/	/j/	/Ch/

Card 8

/g/	/w/	/d/	/Ng/
/n/	/h/	/Ch/	/m/
/k/	/r/	/l/	/s/
/z/	/j/	/t/	/p/

What mouse won't eat cheese?
A computer mouse

Chapter One   Consonant Sounds Bingo   Consonants

/Ng/	/n/	/p/	/TH/
/t/	/h/	/m/	/l/
/f/	/j/	/v/	/Sh/
/z/	/ch/	/zh/	/r/

9

/s/	/g/	/Th/	/p/
/f/	/sh/	/w/	/Ng/
/b/	/v/	/l/	/y/
/d/	/k/	/zh/	/m/

10

/g/	/s/	/d/	/w/
/r/	/Th/	/l/	/h/
/j/	/zh/	/b/	/k/
/ch/	/v/	/TH/	/m/

11

/h/	/z/	/g/	/s/
/y/	/n/	/Th/	/zh/
/TH/	/f/	/p/	/Sh/
/r/	/j/	/w/	/t/

12

 If 2 is company and 3 is a crowd, what are 4 and 5?
9

Chapter One Consonant Sounds Bingo Consonants

Card 13

/k/	/d/	/h/	/z/
/y/	/t/	/f/	/Sh/
/l/	/Ng/	/n/	/Th/
/b/	/v/	/g/	/f/

Card 14

/k/	/g/	/p/	/Ng/
/Sh/	/Zh/	/h/	/b/
/j/	/Ch/	/d/	/r/
/f/	/Th/	/l/	/TH/

Card 15

/TH/	/y/	/h/	/j/
/b/	/r/	/v/	/Ng/
/z/	/Zh/	/k/	/n/
/l/	/s/	/d/	/p/

Card 16

/v/	/b/	/r/	/g/
/m/	/k/	/Th/	/t/
/j/	/y/	/f/	/Sh/
/w/	/Sh/	/s/	/n/

Where did people dance in medieval times?
Knight clubs

© Judy Thompson 2011

Chapter One · Consonant Sounds Bingo · Consonants

/t/	/m/	/z/	/Zh/
/p/	/j/	/f/	/v/
/w/	/CH/	/y/	/h/
/Ng/	/d/	/Sh/	/r/

17

/CH/	/Zh/	/h/	/b/
/k/	/s/	/TH/	/j/
/Ng/	/l/	/g/	/t/
/r/	/Th/	/v/	/z/

18

/l/	/s/	/h/	/t/
/n/	/Zh/	/w/	/m/
/d/	/y/	/f/	/Th/
/j/	/TH/	/v/	/k/

19

/w/	/Ng/	/Sh/	/p/
/z/	/b/	/g/	/CH/
/f/	/m/	/n/	/s/
/y/	/r/	/k/	/j/

20

What has a lot of keys but cannot open any doors?
A piano

Fly Swatter Game – What's the Symbol?

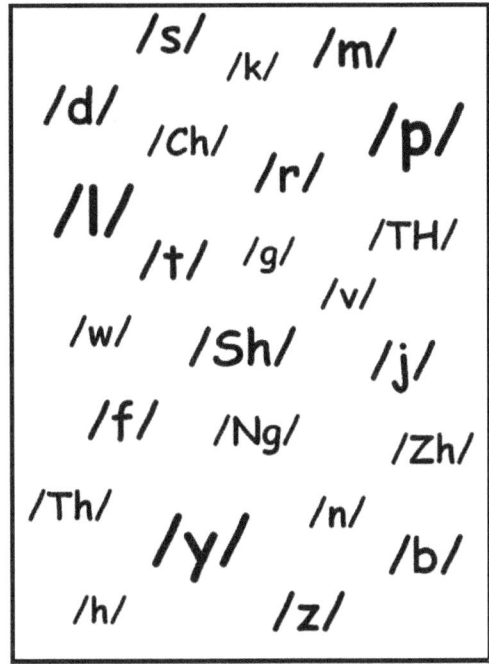

I was introduced to this style of activity at a conference and it looked like fun – that said, I never actually used it in a class of my own – mostly because I hate distinguishing winners and losers. However, some teachers are really good at managing competitive classroom games, so I have included this exercise for them.

Transfer the above **Consonant Sound Board** or something similar to a big piece of Bristol board and mount it on the classroom wall.

Materials: Large **Consonant Sound Board**, two ordinary fly swatters and a word list (any of the Bingo word lists or a list of vocabulary you are working on in class will do.)

Instructions: Have the students stand and form two lines (teams) facing the **Consonant Sound Board**. The first student in each line holds a flyswatter. When the teacher calls out a word from the word list, these students slap the fly swatter on the symbol they believe that word begins with. The first student to slap the correct EPA for the first sound in the word gets a point for their team. Add up the points to determine the winning team.

Take it easy – it's all fun and games until someone loses an eye!

Consonant Silliness

Tongue Twisters sung to the Battle Hymn of the Republic
(Glory Glory Hallelujah)

Black Bug
As one black bug bled blue black blood, the other black bug bled blue.
As one black bug bled blue black blood, the other black bug bled blue.
As one black bug bled blue black blood, the other black bug bled blue.
As one black bug bled blue black blood, the other black bug bled blue.

Rapid Rabbit
As one rapid rabbit ran up the ramp, the other rapid rabbit ran down.
As one rapid rabbit ran up the ramp, the other rapid rabbit ran down.
As one rapid rabbit ran up the ramp, the other rapid rabbit ran down.
As one rapid rabbit ran up the ramp, the other rapid rabbit ran down.

Slimy Snake
As one slimy snake slid up the slough, the other slimy snake slid down.
As one slimy snake slid up the slough, the other slimy snake slid down.
As one slimy snake slid up the slough, the other slimy snake slid down.
As one slimy snake slid up the slough, the other slimy snake slid down.

Then there is this old chestnut:

Peter Piper
Peter Piper picked a peck of pickled peppers;
A peck of pickled peppers Peter Piper picked;
If Peter Piper picked a peck of pickled peppers,
Where's the peck of pickled peppers Peter Piper picked?

Try saying these quickly three times:

Gene and Jerry jumped into the jeep.

Rubber baby buggy bumpers

She sells sea shells by the seashore.

Wendy walks to work on Wednesdays.

Theodore thinks Thursday is the thirtieth.

Cry Wolf

Once upon a time, a lonely shepherd boy sat watching his sheep. Nothing unusual ever happened on the quiet hillside, so the boy decided to play a trick on the townspeople. He cried, *Wolf! Wolf! Wolf!* The villagers ran up the hill armed with sticks to drive the wolf away. There was no wolf.

Everyone was angry that the boy was just pulling their leg, but the boy enjoyed his little joke. The next day he cried, *Wolf! Wolf! The wolf is eating the sheep!* Again the villagers ran to help. The boy laughed at them.

On the third day, a big hungry wolf attacked the sheep. The terrified boy screamed for help, but no one came. The wolf ate all the sheep. The boy realized too late the importance of telling the truth.

Sound Search – Consonants

Search the story for examples of consonant sounds. Put one or two examples beside each EPA sound symbol. The first one is done for you. (Solution is on page 221.)

/b/	boy, big, but	/s/	_____
/d/	_____	/t/	_____
/f/	_____	/v/	_____
/g/	_____	/w/	_____
/h/	_____	/y/	_____
/j/	_____	/z/	_____
/k/	_____	/sh/	_____
/l/	_____	/ch/	_____
/m/	_____	/TH/	_____
/n/	_____	/Th/	_____
/p/	_____	/Ng/	_____
/r/	_____	/zh/	_____

Why are sheep bad dog trainers?

Because ewe can't teach an old dog new tricks.

Chapter Two

VOWELS

Vowels were something else. He didn't like them and they didn't like him. There were only five of them, but they seemed to be everywhere. Why, you could go through twenty words without bumping into some of the shyer consonants, but it seemed as if you couldn't tiptoe past a syllable without waking up a vowel. Consonants, you know pretty much where you stood, but you could never trust a vowel.

Jerry Spinelli (Maniac Magee)

Vowels

What's the difference between a consonant and a vowel?

I was in a course on Teaching Pronunciation by Katherine Brillinger when she asked that question. I had no idea. Neither did anyone else in the class. We knew examples of consonants and vowels, but we didn't know *why*. What makes a vowel a vowel?

She hooked a big, fat rubber band between her thumbs, pulled her hands apart and said, **Vowels sounds stretch. Eeeeeyyyyyyy**

The Free Online Dictionary entry for *vowel* looks like this:

> vow·el (vou'əl)
> *n.*
> **1.** A speech sound, such as (ē) or (ī), created by the relatively free passage of breath through the larynx and oral cavity, usually forming the most prominent and central sound of a syllable.
> **2.** A letter, such as *a, e, i, o, u,* and sometimes *y* in the English alphabet, that represents a vowel.

I like Katherine's definition better, and I have carried a package of big, fat rubber bands to hand out to my students ever since.

On the next page is the industry standard style of diagram that indicates where in the mouth vowel sounds are created. This has been modified for EPA– I found the key words more helpful than the diagram, but that might be just me.

 ## The Funny Farm

If chickens get up when the rooster crows, when do ducks get up?
The quack of dawn

What do you call the best butter on the farm?
A goat

What has one horn and gives milk?
A milk truck

Why did the farmer name his pig 'Ink'?
Because it kept running out of the pen.

English is Stupid, page 50

EPA Vowel Formation Chart

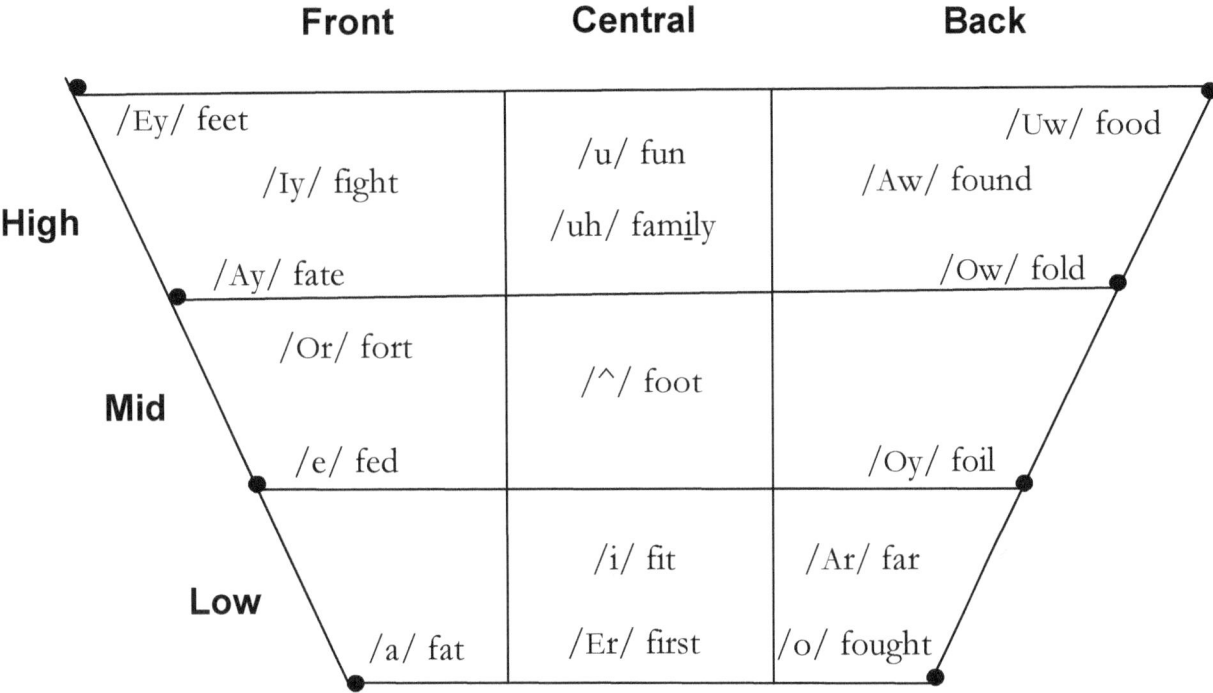

If you look up Vowel Formation Chart on the internet, you will find many diagrams that look a lot like this. The shape is supposed to represent the inside of a human mouth, the left side being the front of the mouth and the right being the back.

These diagrams are supposed to help people create or say specific vowel sounds by showing them where in the mouth the sound is generated. I think they are silly, and I have never personally used one in a classroom as it is difficult to relate the geometric diagram to the sounds in any meaningful way. I have never seen one that has the sounds in the right place – **until this one!**

We have modified the chart to include the phonetic symbol for the sound as well as a sample word showcasing the vowel sound. Since this type of chart is an industry standard, we have included it in case someone out there trying to learn English might find it helpful.

If you like this kind of tool, this is the best one there is. Knock yourself out.

 *Always end the name of your child with a vowel, so that when you yell, the name will carry.*
— *Bill Cosby*

Vowels

In English, the relationship between consonant symbols and consonant sounds is very weak; the relationship between vowel symbols and vowel sounds is nonexistent.

Let's go with *five* for the number of vowels in English – **a, e, i, o, u**. They represent sixteen different vowel sounds. This is a huge problem. It is much easier for students if you are completely honest with them and say, **Any vowel can represent any vowel sound at any time. There are no rules**. There is no *i before e* or *when two vowels go a walking*. Vowels can make *any* sound at *any* time. It is devastating and scary, but it is always easier to deal with the truth.

After you have whipped the rug out from under their feet, you must instantly reassure them that you can fix it. And you can. So let's get to it.

For some reason, everyone learns the names of colors first when they are learning a new language. This is extremely important because each of the sixteen vowel sounds in English can be found in the English names for ordinary colors.

This is important because students can remember words by their vowel color and don't have to rely on (unreliable) spelling to know how a word is going to sound.

 This explanation may be hard to follow, but it will become clearer with an example. There is a video lesson on the sound/color relationship on our website, www.ThompsonLanguageCenter.com, and the dialogue goes like this:

Hold up a plain gray piece of cardboard and ask the class:

> **What color is this?**

Someone will softly say, **Gray.**

> **That's right!**

Repeat the word: **gray, gray, gray, gray, gray** as you turn the card around.

> **Can you hear the sound /Ay/ inside the word gray?**

/Ay/

Students will nod or say yes.

> **Awesome. Can you think of any other words with the sound /Ay/ in them?**

Students will typically offer **May** and **play. That's right!**

English is Stupid, page 52

Take their contributions and write them on the board, all the while making sure a variety of spellings of the /Ay/ sound get on the board, too. Soon you have a list that looks something like this:

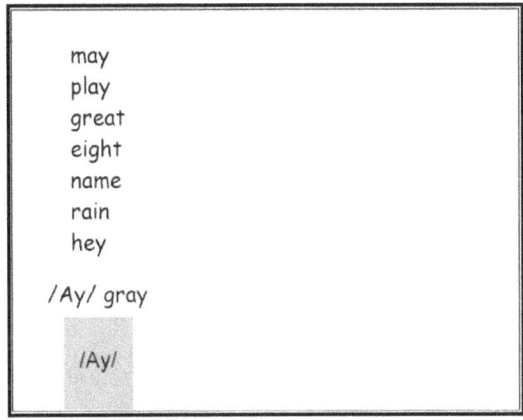

The room will be very quiet as the students stare at different spellings of the same sound.

It doesn't matter anymore how these words are spelled. They can be remembered as gray words.

What color is rain?

A student will answer: gray.

What color is great?	Lots of students will answer:	gray.
What color is play?	More students will answer:	gray.
What color is name?	All students will answer:	gray!

The students have just learned how to pronounce a word from its color – **not its spelling.**

Then hold up a black card and say: What color is this?

And so on…

The rain in Spain falls mainly on the plain.

A fun way of showing this sound is a vocal exercise for /Ay/ from *My Fair Lady*. Take a look at this video on youtube: http://www.youtube.com/watch?v=uVmU3iANbgk

 Why was the cheese shredder cheered on stage?
He was grate.

English is Stupid, page 53

Thompson Vowel Chart

Color Word	Color	EPA	Phonetic Spelling	Example
gray		/Ay/	/grAy/	made
black		/a/	/blak/	mad
green		/Ey/	/grEyn/	Pete
red		/e/	/red/	pet
white		/Iy/	/wIyt/	bite
pink		/i/	/piNgk/	bit
gold		/Ow/	/gOwld/	note
olive		/o/	/oliv/	not
blue		/Uw/	/blUw/	cute
mustard		/u/	/mustErd/	cut
wood		/^/	/w^d/	good
turquoise		/Oy/	/tErkOyz/	boy
brown		/Aw/	/brAwn/	cow
purple		/Er/	/pErpul/	girl
charcoal		/Ar/	/chArkOwl/	car
orange		/Or/	/Orenj/	door

The Most Powerful Speaking Exercise that Ever Existed

I am not kidding! The rest of the book is filler, so don't step over this one. The *Blank Thompson Vowel Chart Exercise* on the following page is the most powerful exercise students will ever participate in. The whole class contributes, which is juicy and fun. It takes about 20 minutes of just being with the paper and the sounds, which is reinforcing. When they are finished, everyone in the class will own a single piece of paper that tells them how to pronounce every word in the English language. I just want to be absolutely clear about how important this exercise is.

Here is how the exercise works.

> Copy enough of the blank Color Charts for every student, plus a few extra for good measure.
>
> Hand a light gray-colored pencil and the whole pile of copies to the first student. This student is to color the first section in the "Color" column gray, then pass the sheet to the next student. The first student then continues to color only the first square on all the other copies, one page at a time, before passing the page to the next student. I usually mention Henry Ford and production lines at this time.
>
> Give the second student a black-colored pencil. This student is to color in the second square and hand the paper to the third student, who has a green pencil, and so on …

There are over a million words in the English language, and every one of them is only one color. When students learn a new word, they automatically begin to file the word into the color/sound it makes.

Why this is so amazing!

For example, the /i/ sound in *it, is, with, sister* and *Miss* is **pink**. When students learn the **pink** sound, they can pronounce tricky words like *women, build* and *busy* correctly without having to hear them a hundred times. They don't need to hear the words at all; they only need to know they are **pink**, and trained students will say /wimen/ and /bild/ correctly out loud without prompting – **and they feel great about it!**

Staples home brand has a good set of colored pencils – the olive, mustard and turquoise colors are the hardest to match in other sets.

 A set of 8½" x 11" *Color Vowel Cards* is available to purchase from the E-store at ThompsonLanguageCenter.com. Also on the website are sample videos of how this lesson works.

English is Stupid, page 55

Blank Thompson Vowel Chart

Color Word	Color	EPA	Phonetic Spelling	Example	Example with 'f'
gray		/Ay/	/grAy/	made	face
black		/a/	/blak/	mad	fast
green		/Ey/	/grEyn/	Pete	feel
red		/e/	/red/	pet	fell
white		/Iy/	/wIyt/	bite	file
pink		/i/	/piNgk/	bit	fill
gold		/Ow/	/gOwld/	note	fold
olive		/o/	/oliv/	not	fall
blue		/Uw/	/blUw/	cute	food
mustard		/u/	/mustErd/	cut	fun
wood		/^/	/w^d/	put	full
turquoise		/Oy/	/tErkOyz/	boy	foil
brown		/Aw/	/brAwn/	cow	found
purple		/Er/	/pErpul/	word	first
charcoal		/Ar/	/chArkOwl/	car	far
orange		/Or/	/Orenj/	door	four

Different Ways to Spell the Same Vowel Sound

FYI Reference Sheet

EPA	Examples
/ Ay /	gray, grey, day, eight, hey, rain, steak, café, soufflé, sundae
/ a /	black, plaid, laugh, half
/ Ey /	green, seat, machine, ski, piece, me, candy, people, quay
/ e /	red, head, said, guess, friend
/ Iy /	white, height, I, my, eye, aye, aisle, choir, pie
/ i /	pink, pretty, busy, build, women
/ Ow /	gold, note, go, boat, toe, sew, know, though, mauve
/ o /	olive, father, cough, taught, crawl
/ Uw /	blue, cute, two, do, who, through, new, too, shoe, glue, juice
/ u /	mustard, mother, was, the, cousin, because, flood
/ ^ /	wood, could, put, woman
/ Oy /	turquoise, boy, noise, lawyer
/ Aw /	brown, house, vowel
R Vowels	
/ Er /	purple, her, were, shirt, certain, nurse, word, earth
/ Ar /	charcoal, heart, R
/ Or /	orange, door, more, pour, war, for, drawer

Why did the student nibble on her calendar?
She wanted a sundae.

English is Stupid, page 226

Chapter Two English Phonetic Alphabet Workbook Vowels

ESL Telephone Alphabet Colors

A ace	B boy	C cat
D dog	E east	F five
G goat	H house	I ice cream
J July	K king	L lemon
M money	N number	O open
P people	Q queen	R red
S summer	T time	U uniform
V visa	W woman	X x-ray
Y yellow	Z zebra	

Exercise: What color are the words in the ESL Telephone Alphabet? (Solution is on page 222.)

A ace _gray_	B boy _____	C cat _____
D dog _____	E east _____	F five _____
G goat _____	H house _____	I ice cream _____
J July _____	K king _____	L lemon _____
M money _____	N number _____	O open _____
P people _____	Q queen _____	R red _____
S summer _____	T time _____	U uniform _____
V visa _____	W woman _____	X x-ray _____
Y yellow _____	Z zebra _____	

When is a boy not a boy?

When he turns into a candy store.

© Judy Thompson 2011

Er – Ar – Or Pronunciation

Put a check mark beside each word under its vowel sound: **Purple, Charcoal** or **Orange**. (Solution is on page 222.)

	/Er/	/Ar/	/Or/
shirt	✓	___	___
park	___	___	___
door	___	___	___
warm	___	___	___
store	___	___	___
sugar	___	___	___
alarm	___	___	___
court	___	___	___
normal	___	___	___
herd	___	___	___
organ	___	___	___
heart	___	___	___
earth	___	___	___
turn	___	___	___
storm	___	___	___
certain	___	___	___
curtain	___	___	___
worth	___	___	___

Rhyming Words for Every Color

Find words that rhyme with the sample word in each row. (Solution is on page 222.)

	Sound	Example						
1	/Ay/	fate						
2	/a/	fat						
3	/Ey/	feet						
4	/e/	fed						
5	/Iy/	fight						
6	/i/	fit						
7	/Ow/	fold						
8	/o/	fought						
9	/Uw/	food						
10	/u/	fun						
11	/^/	foot						
12	/Oy/	foil						
13	/Aw/	found						
14	/Er/	first						
15	/Ar/	far						
16	/Or/	four						

Listening Speaking Skills Instructions

These are covered in detail on page 38.

There is also a video clip on the www.ThompsonLanguageCenter.com website.

If you haven't already been using this fantastic speaking tool, please take a look. If you took the opportunity in Chapter One to teach your class how this drill works, you'll be very glad you did because this time it is going to go much faster.

The instructions for the Listening Speaking Skill activity are on page 38, including a sample teacher (page 39).

 **Knock-Knock Jokes**

Knock, Knock!
    Who's there?
Boo!
    Boo who?
Don't cry, it's only an English lesson.

    Knock, Knock!
        Who's there?
    July!
        July who?
    July or tell the truth.

Knock, Knock!
    Who's there?
Beef!
    Beef who?
Beef-ore I tell you, let me come in!

    Knock, Knock!
        Who's there?
    Cook!
        Cook who?
    Hey! Who are you calling cuckoo!

Green /ɛy/, Red /e/, Pink /i/

	1	2	3	4	5	Student A 6	7	8	9	10	Student B 11	12	13	14	15
beat															
bit															
seat															
sit															
neat															
net															
meat															
met															
bet															
bit															
set															
sit															
net															
knit															
met															
mitt															
beat															
bet															
seat															
set															
neat															
knit															
meat															
mitt															

Gray /ay/, Black /a/, Red /e/

	1	2	3	4	5	Student A 6	7	8	9	10	Student B 11	12	13	14	15
made															
mad															
Kate															
cat															
cane															
can															
played															
plaid															
raid															
red															
stayed															
stead															
wade															
wed															
shade															
shed															
had															
head															
gas															
guess															
pat															
pet															
jam															
gem															

Chapter Two   Listening Speaking Skills   Vowels

White/Pink, Gold/Olive, Blue/Mustard

	1	2	3	4	5	Student A 6 7 8 9 10	Student B 11 12 13 14 15
site							
sit							
night							
knit							
fine							
fin							
eyes							
is							
note							
not							
boat							
bought							
phone							
fawn							
bowl							
ball							
boot							
but							
roof							
ruff							
tune							
ton							
dune							
done							

Purple /ɛr/, Charcoal /ɑr/, Orange /ɔr/

	1	2	3	4	5	Student A 6	7	8	9	10	Student B 11	12	13	14	15
perk															
park															
stir															
star															
burn															
barn															
hurt															
heart															
were															
war															
firm															
form															
turn															
torn															
curse															
course															
far															
for															
part															
port															
cart															
court															
lard															
lord															

Circle the Words that Rhyme
Basic

Circle the groups of words that rhyme. (Solution is on page 223.)

(eight	to	street
ate)	no	heat
date)	go	feet

rose	four	good
hose	door	hood
toes	more	food

nut	guest	bread
cut	test	bead
put	best	bed

C	now	kiss
he	not	miss
three	cow	hiss

sign	you	bought
mine	blue	right
whine	knew	caught

park	oil	bird
perk	boil	word
mark	royal	third

 What do you call an average seamstress?
So-sew

English is Stupid, page 67

Circle the Words that Rhyme
Advanced

Circle the groups of words that rhyme. (Solution is on page 223.)

(ache / break / make) heard pair
 beard bear
 feared beer

hairy come suit
very from suite
marry gum sweet

worst her fuel
first were school
versed there who'll

eye could back
why wood plaque
ski should yak

said with boat
fed myth wrote
head south vote

knot oil mouth
lot royal south
thought foil youth

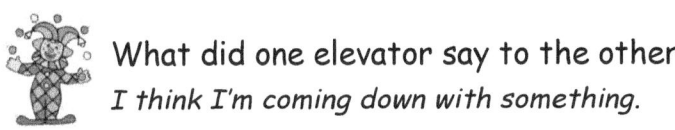

What did one elevator say to the other?
I think I'm coming down with something.

English is Stupid, page 67

Homonym Horrors

Circle the correct word that best completes each sentence. (Solution is on page 223.)

1. Would you please **(grate, great)** the cheese for the pizza?
2. **(Wait, weight)** for me! There's a **(not, knot)** in my shoelaces.
3. Brennan chopped **(wood, would)** in the spring for the following winter.
4. Granny fills a **(pale, pail)** with rainwater to water her flowers.
5. John's guitar **(lessen, lesson)** is on Wednesdays every **(weak, week)**.
6. It was a bad **(brake, break)** and took a long time to **(heel, heal)**.
7. Morgan's voice was a little **(hoarse, horse)** from her sore throat.
8. The car had a flat tire so he had it **(towed, toad)**.
9. **(You're, Your)** purse is on the desk by the door.
10. Toys away, kids! It's bath time; leave your **(bare, bear)** behind.
11. Diane liked to **(sew, so)** her own **(close, clothes)** to save money.
12. Ayden's **(manners, manors)** are excellent. He is **(so, sew)** polite.
13. You'll never **(no, know)** how much **(eye, I)** love you.
14. That barking dog drives me nuts. It's a **(pain, pane)** in the neck.
15. Things will work out – take it **(won, one)** day at a **(time, thyme)**.
16. The **(ants, aunts)** go marching **(to, two) (buy, by) (to, two)**, hurrah, hurrah.
17. It's a **(fair, fare)** price for a used car.
18. When you **(idle, idol)** your car at the drive-through, it hurts the environment.
19. Tell me the story of the tortoise and the **(hair, hare)**.
20. Ryan is taking a trip down the **(isle, aisle, I'll)** on October 14.

 ESL student: **Could I have some bread?**

Baker: **No, I knead it.**

Mystery Word Match Series

Here is another **Mystery Word Match Series** because **I love them**!

There is a basic and an advanced **Mystery Word Match** for each of the 16 vowel sounds.

The basic level uses simpler words and explanations but still includes a variety of spellings for the featured vowel sound.

The advanced level uses higher vocabulary, trickier concepts and more difficult explanations.

For the lowest levels, study the vocabulary beforehand and give the exercise to the students in groups. Higher-level beginners may work in pairs. To make the same exercise more difficult for intermediate students, cover the answer box at the bottom of the page when photocopying. Depending on the class, students may work in groups, pairs or on their own with the answers available or not.

(Solutions begin on page 224.)

 **Riddle Me This**

What word starts with e, ends with e, and only has one letter in it?
Envelope

What is more useful after it's broken
An egg

What can fall down and never get hurt?
Snow

How far can you walk into the woods?
Half way – then you are walking out.

What side of a cake is the right side?
The side that gets eaten because the other side is left.

Gray /Ay/ – Basic

What word with /Ay/ answers the statements below?

1.	Words a person is known by that make up their signature	
2.	She takes food orders and brings food in a restaurant.	
3.	Thin white sheets of writing material made from trees	
4.	Description of pain in the stomach, head, ear, back or tooth	
5.	Thick, flat cut of beef that is tasty cooked on the barbeque	
6.	Eyes, nose, mouth and cheeks are all parts of this body part.	
7.	Sweet, dark brown fruit from a palm tree; or notations on a calendar	
8.	Red, orange, yellow, green, blue, violet arc in the sky on a sunny/rainy day.	
9.	Shiny metal, fancy-colored jewellery worn on women's arms	
10.	A cozy little restaurant for meeting friends and drinking coffee	
11.	Passenger and freight transportation with cars pulled by an engine on steel tracks	
12.	A short rest for 15 minutes in the middle of the morning	
13.	Stand on a scale to measure heaviness in pounds or kilos	
14.	This day, the day between yesterday and tomorrow	

date	bracelet	name	break
train	ache	cafe	waitress
today	steak	paper	face
rainbow	weigh		

Gray /Ay/ – Advanced

What word with /Ay/ answers the statements below?

1.	Oats, wheat, barley and sorghum that grow on the prairies	
2.	Another name for surgery, a medical procedure performed in a hospital	
3.	Direction forward without turning left or right	
4.	Guardian spirit depicted with a halo and wings	
5.	Circular dial that indicates the amount of gas, air pressure or engine temperature	
6.	Earth's largest continent, home to the highest number of people	
7.	An adjective or noun that refers to the way animals (including humans) act	
8.	Reptile without legs that propels itself by slithering	
9.	The total number of individuals that live in a country	
10.	The blood vessel that takes oxygen-depleted blood back to the heart	
11.	Develop an idea, object or process that never existed before	
12.	Two-dimensional shape with four sides of equal length	
13.	Families that live in your community, the nearest on either side of your house.	
14.	*Gray matter*, the spongy vital organ in the head protected by the skull	

create	grain	Asia	operation
snake	square	population	angel
straight	gauge	behavior	vein
neighbor	brain		

Chapter Two — Mystery Word Match — Vowels

Black /ɑ/ – Basic

What word with /ɑ/ answers the statements below?

1.	Green, red or yellow juicy round fruit from a tree	
2.	Noise people make when they hear something funny	
3.	Green ground-cover that grows wild or is trimmed in yards as lawn	
4.	Muscular part of the leg below the knee; a baby cow is called the same word.	
5.	Fashion accessory for keeping a head warm in winter	
6.	Contraction or short form of cannot	
7.	The final place; the position you don't want to finish in a race	
8.	Set of rules especially important for written English that includes noun, verb, adjective, etc.	
9.	Group of people headed by a parent or parents that includes children and other blood relatives	
10.	Respond to a question; what to do when the phone rings	
11.	Movement to music that is personally, artistically or culturally expressive	
12.	Long, sweet yellow tropical fruit that grows in bunches	
13.	Four fingers, a thumb and a palm are the main parts of this extremity	
14.	Sounds, words and gestures people use to communicate	

last	banana	hat	calf
family	grammar	laugh	dance
language	apple	answer	can't
grass	hand		

© Judy Thompson 2011

Black /a/ – Advanced

What word with /a/ answers the statements below?

1.	Assembly line institution where products are manufactured	
2.	The great continent with the Sahara, Congo and the Serengeti	
3.	Statistics and their relationships are depicted on this style of scaled diagram	
4.	Circular strip of stretchy rubber perfect for demonstrating vowel action	
5.	English has a Latin one of these for writing and the EPA for speaking	
6.	Tartan pattern from Scotland with colorful stripes running up and down, side to side	
7.	Vast collection of words studied to learn a new language	
8.	Lunch favorite with sliced meat, tuna fish, chopped eggs or peanut butter between two slices of bread	
9.	Rake fingernails back and forth over an itchy rash	
10.	I see. I know what you mean. I _ _ _ _ _ _ _ _ _ _ .	
11.	Professional office building cleaner or school custodian	
12.	Shorten a verb by replacing a letter with an apostrophe	
13.	Back massage, tranquilizers and beach holidays are different ways to do the same thing	
14.	A topic in mathematics that studies parts of a whole	

relax	elastic	janitor	vocabulary
understand	factory	plaid	sandwich
alphabet	scratch	graph	contraction
Africa	fractions		

Green /Ey/ – Basic

What word with /Ey/ answers the statements below?

1.	Popular drink served hot, cold, black, green and herbal	
2.	Long green vegetable that looks like a cucumber and starts with a z	
3.	Adults need eight hours of this and children need even more every day	
4.	Local and regional law enforcement officers	
5.	Dentists advise brushing these *pearly whites* after every meal	
6.	Personal happiness and international harmony	
7.	Achoo! Direct this cold/allergy symptom into your elbow.	
8.	Black and white striped African animal is a cousin of the horse	
9.	Small cut metallic object to unlock doors and start cars	
10.	Made from denim, they are the most popular garment in the world.	
11.	Small piece of paper cashiers give to prove the bill is paid	
12.	Gender that includes nanny, mare, ewe, hen and woman	
13.	Effortless, as in the expression as _ _ _ _ as pie	
14.	Section of something bigger, like a slice of cake	

easy	zucchini	peace	female
police	receipt	sleep	sneeze
jeans	teeth	key	tea
piece	zebra		

Green /Ey/ – Advanced

What word with /Ey/ answers the statements below?

1.	Someone with an intelligence quotient (IQ) higher than 140 points	
2.	A piece of manufacturing equipment that allows fewer men to get more work done	
3.	Oily substance for frying food or lubricating metal parts	
4.	Plural of person, a collection of two or more individuals	
5.	Prioritizing of emergency patients in a hospital ward according to severity of injuries	
6.	Educated professional who uses calculations to design bridges and equipment	
7.	Downhill or cross-country winter sport enthusiasts enjoy this at snow-covered resorts	
8.	Inhale of oxygen and exhale of carbon monoxide using the nose, lungs, etc.	
9.	Form of electronic messaging that has replaced letter writing and other business communication	
10.	Certificate of completion from a college or university	
11.	Popular but very hot member of the pepper family	
12.	Stimulant ingested in chocolate, coffee, cola or black tea	
13.	Have faith in an idea or set of religious doctrines	
14.	Organized sports teams that compete regularly following a posted schedule	

machine	league	email	caffeine
engineer	genius	skiing	jalapeno
grease	people	triage	breathe
believe	degree		

Chapter Two — Mystery Word Match — Vowels

Red /e/ – Basic

What word with /e/ answers the statements below?

1.	The second month of the year is also the shortest with only 28 days	
2.	Small sweet red fruit on top of an ice cream sundae	
3.	Loaves of this baked food are sliced to make sandwiches	
4.	The sunny color of daffodils, lemons and bananas	
5.	What a person becomes when their first child is born	
6.	A close pal who is not a family member	
7.	The final position, or the last word in a folk tale	
8.	The irregular past tense of the verb **say**	
9.	Postal workers deliver these in envelopes with stamps.	
10.	Made from copper, stamped with the year it was minted, it's the smallest unit of money.	
11.	A distinguishing feature of a bird, its coat is made of hundreds of these.	
12.	Soft-spoken and kind, an adjective that compares someone to a lamb	
13.	In the olden days, school started when this rang.	
14.	The host or hostess says, *Make yourself at home* to this visitor.	

bell	parent	feathers	bread
said	cherry	penny	letters
end	gentle	February	guest
friend	yellow		

© Judy Thompson 2011 — www.ThompsonLanguageCenter.com

Red /e/ – Advanced

What word with /e/ answers the statements below?

1.	One milk and one sugar in a black coffee	
2.	Physically fit; of sound mind and body; full of vim and vigour	
3.	Not sure of the correct answer, but take a stab at one anyway	
4.	Wedding ceremony and registry of the process of two people who enter into holy matrimony	
5.	Bienvenue, salve, willkommen, bienvenido	
6.	Winter solstice, yuletide and *Seasons Greetings* fall during this chilly month	
7.	With a special map, pirates seek this buried oak chest full of gold doubloons.	
8.	Household appliances plug into wall sockets that provide this source of energy.	
9.	Better than great, an absolutely fantastic piece of work	
10.	Unspecific number of things, much more than a few	
11.	Pay this and get more out of your lessons; you'll learn English faster and your teacher will be happy.	
12.	Made from the hides of animals, this tanned material makes beautiful coats, purses and couches.	
13.	A professional; one who knows a tremendous amount about their field	
14.	One short of a dozen; rhymes with seven	

guess	electricity	marriage	treasure
excellent	healthy	attention	regular
December	eleven	expert	many
leather	welcome		

Chapter Two — Mystery Word Match — Vowels

White /ɪy/ – Basic

What word with /ɪy/ answers the statements below?

1.	Female spouse, the woman married to the husband	
2.	The word is only one letter, the first person singular pronoun, and it is always capitalized	
3.	Deep expression of emotion that requires tissues for falling tears and running noses	
4.	The measure of tallness in feet and inches or centimetres	
5.	Generic term for human offspring, either a son or a daughter	
6.	An adjective that means thoughtful and starts with *k*	
7.	Number of rings in the official symbol of the Olympic games	
8.	Pupil, iris, cornea and lens are parts of this sight organ	
9.	The same word is the opposite of *left* and *wrong*	
10.	Round, flaky, fruit-filled pastry served as a popular dessert	
11.	First person possessive, the coat belongs to me, it's ___ coat.	
12.	Informal greeting, a very short form of *hello*	
13.	The last word said that marks the end of a conversation	
14.	Above the knee, it's the thick muscular top part of the leg.	

hi	kind	height	child
wife	bye	pie	I
thigh	right	five	my
eye	cry		

© Judy Thompson 2011

White /Iy/ – Advanced

What word with /Iy/ answers the statements below?

1.	Piece of land completely surrounded by water	
2.	Tropical fruit that looks like a longish melon with orange flesh and black seeds	
3.	Long, thin spears of frozen water hanging from the eaves in winter	
4.	Cyber destination indicated by a URL address	
5.	A characteristic of poetry that has phrases end with similar sounds	
6.	Long numbered hallway in the grocery store lined with shelves stocked with food	
7.	Environmental impact program that repurposes used products	
8.	Clarity, cut and color determine the quality and value of this precious gem	
9.	Librarians insist on complete absence of sound at all times	
10.	Versatile synthetic material that can be thin enough for raincoats or substantial enough to be floor covering	
11.	An organized group of singers that regularly perform as part of a church service	
12.	Information source for times, content, titles and durations of television programming	
13.	Something unexpected, either good like a present or bad like a co-worker suddenly quitting his/her job	
14.	A low-growing aromatic herb of the mint family that is delicious with lamb	

choir	aisle	thyme	vinyl
surprise	diamond	quiet	recycle
rhyme	icicle	island	papaya
website	guide		

Chapter Two — Mystery Word Match — Vowels

Pink /i/ – Basic

What word with /i/ answers the statements below?

1.	Coldest season that begins on the solstice, December 21	
2.	More than one youngster, the offspring of parents	
3.	A common adjective that means small or tiny	
4.	Short successive *beep beep beep* sounds on the phone indicating the line is _____	
5.	Romantic or affectionate smacking of the lips	
6.	Female sibling, it rhymes with mister	
7.	Two or more adult female human beings	
8.	An urban center with tall buildings and dense population	
9.	Type of book or television show that reveals the villain through a series of clues	
10.	A beautifully wrapped present given at a special occasion like Christmas, birthday or baby shower	
11.	The only way to learn how to speak English	
12.	Occupation, work or trade where money is exchanged for goods and services	
13.	Four slender jointed digits on each hand – not including the thumb	
14.	Totalling two or more numbers together	

gift	adding	siblings	busy
little	sister	mystery	city
women	business	fingers	kiss
winter	listen		

Pink /i/ – Advanced

What word with /i/ answers the statements below?

1.	Generic term for a either a brother or a sister	
2.	Verb synonymous with construct/make, as in construct or make a house	
3.	Quickly closing then opening one eye in a saucy fashion	
4.	Traditional scores of religious music performed weekly in church	
5.	The taxman wants to know the total amount of money made over the year	
6.	Warm, wet growing season; tight steel squashy coil	
7.	The verb for officially putting a home up for sale with a real estate agent	
8.	An adjective describing a beautiful woman or a slangy measure of about 70% as in, *He's a _____ nice guy*.	
9.	Create a piercing sound to cheer for a performance or beckon a dog by forcing air between pursed lips to	
10.	Poison ivy causes these itchy red pockets of fluid under the skin	
11.	Ancient tale of a fantastic exploit that isn't literally true	
12.	Three-dimensional circle, the shape of a toilet paper roll	
13.	What a person thinks about a situation, not always based on fact. Everyone has a right to their own.	
14.	Rivalry, either casually between friends over school grades or formally as in organized sports	

myth	wink	whistle	pretty
list	blisters	income	cylinder
spring	hymns	sibling	build
opinion	competition		

Chapter Two — Mystery Word Match — Vowels

Gold /ow/ – Basic

What word with /ow/ answers the statements below?

1.	Slices of bread, browned on both sides served warm for breakfast	
2.	Make or mend clothing with a needle and thread	
3.	There are five of these digits on the end of each foot	
4.	The purity of this precious metal is stamped in karats	
5.	A child's riding mount; a smaller version of a horse	
6.	Professional baseball pitchers get paid a lot of money to do this with a baseball.	
7.	When something is complete with no pieces missing	
8.	Sign in the window of a store available for business	
9.	Muscular tube inside the neck for swallowing food	
10.	Raw ingredients mixed together prior to baking cookies or bread	
11.	The action of pulling a trailer or piece of equipment with a vehicle	
12.	Parka, trench, fur and wool piece of clothing worn over other clothes	
13.	A house is just a building, it is love that makes it _ _ _ _.	
14.	A facial feature that holds up your glasses and helps you breathe.	

coat	toes	open	whole
nose	throw	dough	home
throat	sew	pony	toast
gold	tow		

Gold /Ow/ – Advanced

What word with /Ow/ answers the statements below?

1.	Pretty decoration twisted from ribbon to adorn a present or a little girl's hair	
2.	A camera takes these and stores them on a film or chip	
3.	The large ball and socket joint that connects the arm to the torso	
4.	Seasoned and smoked low-grade sandwich meat processed from beef and other animals	
5.	Rocks, sand and pebbles where the ocean meets land	
6.	*English is Stupid* is the 6-point training guide for this fundamental division of English	
7.	Old-fashioned French word that translates as *admirer* in English and refers to a boyfriend	
8.	Severe lung illness that can follow a cold or flu	
9.	A two-syllable verb that means *to draw near*	
10.	Area designation for specific use, i.e., residential or commercial development	
11.	Halloween falls on the last day of this month.	
12.	Title of a fashion magazine and one of Madonna's hits. It means *in style*.	
13.	A conjunction meaning *in spite of* that introduces surprising information	
14.	Seat of power and actual chair the queen sits in	

coast	photos	beau	although
pneumonia	zone	spoken	bow
vogue	bologna	approach	October
shoulder	throne		

Olive /o/ – Basic

What word with /o/ answers the statements below?

1.	A hot drink enjoyed by adults in the morning	
2.	Female child in a family	
3.	Share ideas and information in normal conversation	
4.	Weekly pile of dark, light and delicate dirty clothes and linen	
5.	Sweet red fruit with its seeds on the outside that grows on rows on the ground	
6.	A good, warm month of the year to take a vacation	
7.	Tasteless, odourless, colorless liquid needed for life	
8.	Legal rule or set of rules enforced by the court system	
9.	Pieces of music played on the radio or sung at home	
10.	Patriarch of the nuclear family, the male parent	
11.	Dense florets that make up a bushy green vegetable	
12.	Cardboard container for cereal, tissue, gifts or shipping merchandize	
13.	Medical practitioner who works at a hospital or clinic	
14.	Patches of cloth sewn on three sides and open at the top to carry things in coats and pants	

songs	strawberry	doctor	pockets
water	daughter	box	broccoli
father	talk	law	coffee
laundry	August		

Chapter Two — Mystery Word Match — Vowels

Olive /o/ – Advanced

What word with /o/ answers the statements below?

1.	The production of goods and services that define the financial state of the country	
2.	Large vegetable with green leaves on the outside and a white *head* on the inside	
3.	Theatrical genre intent on making people laugh	
4.	A noun or verb that has money going into the bank	
5.	The tiny arced punctuation mark that indicates possession	
6.	Past tense synonym for acquire that collocates with a ball, cold or criminal	
7.	What happens to food after it is taken out of the freezer, before it is cooked	
8.	Graduated glass tube of mercury that measures temperature	
9.	Occupation that involves taking pictures for a living	
10.	A doctor who specializes in vision and eyesight	
11.	Awareness or experience of being awake	
12.	Beginning with *th*, it's an idea that forms in one's mind	
13.	A dramatic play presented exclusively through classical music	
14.	Institute of higher learning or education that prepares students for the workforce	

apostrophe	optometrist	economy	thought
deposit	conscious	opera	comedy
thermometer	thaw	photography	caught
college	cauliflower		

Chapter Two — Mystery Word Match — Vowels

Blue /Uw/ – Basic

What word with /Uw/ answers the statements below?

1.	Heavy footwear for a specific purpose, like wet weather or construction work	
2.	The first day of the week that begins with the letter **T**	
3.	Non-count noun that includes apples, melons and pears	
4.	Current events, the local and world reports on TV at 6:00	
5.	Electronic data machine that receives, types and stores information	
6.	Building for education, books, students and teachers	
7.	Two or more students working together in ESL class	
8.	Formal outfit worn by military, postal and law enforcement personnel	
9.	Second person subject pronoun spelled the same in singular and plural forms	
10.	Wild animals are on display for the public in this special place.	
11.	Adjective commonly used by young girls to describe baby animals, handsome boys and shoes	
12.	The answer to this **Wh** question is always a person.	
13.	Formal three-piece set of clothing for business that has at least one pair of pants, a tailored jacket and a vest	
14.	Three syllable word that starts with **b** and describes a gorgeous woman, flower or thing	

boot	you	zoo	Tuesday
suit	fruit	news	school
computer	group	uniform	cute
who	beautiful		

Blue /Uw/ – Advanced

What word with /Uw/ answers the statements below?

1.	Pleasing distant scenery that can increase the value of domestic real estate	
2.	Coal, gas and hydrogen – substance processed and purchased to propel machinery	
3.	A temporarily tender, discolored area of a skin that is the result of an injury	
4.	Fresh squeezed or from concentrate, this fruit product is often consumed at breakfast.	
5.	Underground utility system designed to flush away waste	
6.	Period of years in a person's life prior to maturity	
7.	An adjective indicating approximately two or three	
8.	Highway, course or way of travel from one place to another	
9.	Three dimensional square, the shape of a regular playing dice	
10.	A deputy officer, second in command, the one who could replace the head officer	
11.	Droplets of moisture formed on ground vegetation in the early morning	
12.	Hopping Australian marsupial that carries its young in a pouch	
13.	Preposition that has something moving in one side and out the other	
14.	A favourable opinion; accept as satisfactory	

few	through	view	juice
cube	youth	bruise	route
fuel	sewer	lieutenant	dew
approve	kangaroo		

Chapter Two — Mystery Word Match — Vowels

Mustard /u/ – Basic

What word with /u/ answers the statements below?

1.	Public transit in the city or from city to city	
2.	Units of currency, coins and bills for buying things	
3.	Big orange squash that gets carved into faces at Halloween	
4.	Single, first, alone… all refer to the smallest number	
5.	Bees make this sticky sweet food from the nectar of flowers	
6.	Large organs in the chest responsible for breathing oxygen in and carbon dioxide out	
7.	The son or daughter of a parent's brother or sister	
8.	Sandwiches, fruit, milk and cookies make a healthy meal in the middle of the day	
9.	The Red Cross asks for donations of this vital body fluid	
10.	Nation is another name for a geographical piece of land	
11.	Stick this flexible muscle between the teeth and blow to make the sound /TH/	
12.	The center of our solar system that rises in the east and sets in the west	
13.	Highly irregular past tense form of the verb *to be*	
14.	Romantic feeling of affection or interest stronger than *like*	

love	bus	one	cousin
lungs	blood	was	money
sun	honey	country	lunch
pumpkin	tongue		

© Judy Thompson 2011

Chapter Two — Mystery Word Match — Vowels

Mustard /u/ – Advanced

What word with /u/ answers the statements below?

1.	Kitchen appliance where muffins and tarts are baked	
2.	The elected body that collects taxes in order to run the country	
3.	Jokes and riddles are intended to make people laugh because they are _ _ _ _ _ _ .	
4.	Definate article, the most commonly used word in the English language	
5.	Sufficient to meet a need or adequate to satisfy a want or desire	
6.	The body part under a belt buckle and the organ where food is digested have the same name	
7.	Adverb of frequency when something happens a single time	
8.	Seed of a tulip plant **or** common household light emitting apparatus	
9.	Maternal reference in expressions like _ _ _ _ _ _ _ nature, _ _ _ _ _ _ _ Earth, _ _ _ _ _ _ _ Theresa	
10.	/uv/ in EPA there is neither a **u** or a **v** in the written form of this crazy common little word	
11.	Conjunction that introduces a reason or excuse	
12.	Food that is hard to chew, an exam that is hard to do	
13.	Move toward the person who is speaking **or** an invitation to accompany others on an outing	
14.	Infancy as a relative age or the off-spring of a species	

stomach	enough	once	young
because	bulb	of	mother
oven	government	the	funny
tough	come		

© Judy Thompson 2011 — www.ThompsonLanguageCenter.com

Wood /^/ – Basic

What word with /^/ answers the statements below?

1.	Instruction on the door handle of a public building when it goes away from you	
2.	Past form of the verb take; _ _ _ _ a shower, a nap, a trip, etc.	
3.	She can be any combination of wife, mother, aunt, friend teacher, nurse, sister and more	
4.	Kitchen activity chefs get paid to do and wives don't	
5.	Widely used positive description, as in a well-behaved child is a _ _ _ _ child.	
6.	North Americans call this popular team sport *soccer*	
7.	What the dentist does to remove a bad tooth.	
8.	To view quickly or pay attention to for a short time, a synonym for *see* or *watch*	
9.	A helping verb that is used to give (unwanted) advice	
10.	Bound pages like *English is Stupid* for sale in stores, downloadable or available to borrow from libraries	
11.	A sock keeps this body extremity warm	
12.	White cubes or crystals for naturally sweetening tea and coffee	
13.	Put a worm on this barbed metal device to catch a fish	
14.	Part of a sweatshirt that flips over the head; it covers and protects a car engine	

should	sugar	good	look
book	foot	woman	cook
pull	took	push	football
hook	hood		

Chapter Two — Mystery Word Match — Vowels

Wood /ˆ/ – Advanced

What word with /ˆ/ answers the statements below?

1.	Sheep's hair that is shorn and spun to make sweaters	
2.	Powdery black dirt that coats the inside of chimneys	
3.	Short, thick, prickly vegetation found in gardens and along the sides of the road	
4.	Literally the opposite of *straight* and figuratively a synonym for dishonest	
5.	Large foam-stuffed squares that are the part of the couch for sitting on	
6.	Something a dog says; not a *bark, growl, arf* or *yip*	
7.	An expression for optimists who say the glass is half ____.	
8.	Modal used for polite invitations, permission or possibility	
9.	Chocolate, butterscotch and vanilla are the most common flavours of this creamy dessert	
10.	Past tense of what a baby does to a rattle and what the ground did in the earthquake	
11.	The wild dog-like animal that gave Red Riding Hood so much trouble	
12.	An after-school snack baked with chocolate chips that is delicious with milk	
13.	Waited in line for tickets to the movie	
14.	A versatile little irregular verb that means to *place* or *lay*	

crooked	shook	cushion	woof
put	wolf	wool	full
could	soot	cookie	bush
stood	pudding		

© Judy Thompson 2011 — www.ThompsonLanguageCenter.com

Chapter Two Mystery Word Match Vowels

Turquoise /oy/ – Basic

What word with /oy/ answers the statements below?

1.	The stage of his life after he's a baby, before he's a young man	
2.	Small round metal unit of money in any country	
3.	Special status of the queen and her family	
4.	Loud sound from a party, machinery or barking dog	
5.	Pearl-making, slippery, gray seafood from a hard oval seashell	
6.	Indicate a direction with an extended arm and the index finger	
7.	A professional legal representative who has graduated from law school	
8.	A synonym for happiness that starts with *j*	
9.	Cook food like vegetables and noodles in water on top of the stove	
10.	Flushing washroom fixture improved but not invented by Thomas Crapper in 1881	
11.	Liquid pressed from olives and used for cooking	
12.	A tender cut of meat from the back of a pig or cow	
13.	Brightly-colored play-things usually for children	
14.	Sign up and become a member of a club; connect to things	

oil	joy	royal	point
noise	toys	boy	oyster
join	boil	toilet	loin
lawyer	coin		

Turquoise /oy/ – Advanced

What word with /oy/ answers the statements below?

1.	Earth where seeds are planted and gardens grow	
2.	Hire to work for regular hours in exchange for money	
3.	Mild dampness or tiny bits of water	
4.	Rolls of thin sheets of aluminum to tear off and preserve food	
5.	Medicated topical cream to treat burns and rashes	
6.	Delight in an activity or another person's company	
7.	Stay true to another for a long period of time through difficult circumstances	
8.	Toxic substances that cause ill health or even death	
9.	Break something beyond repair	
10.	Fine needle work with small stitches that decorates cloth	
11.	Celebrate in an extreme state of happiness	
12.	A loud, overbearing, pushy, obnoxious manner	
13.	Continuously bothering someone until they become angry	
14.	Mobile junction of connective tissue between two or more bones	

enjoy	moisture	foil	boisterous
destroy	loyal	employ	rejoice
ointment	embroidery	poison	soil
annoying	joint		

Brown /aw/ – Basic

What word with /aw/ answers the statements below?

1.	Large farm animal that produces much more milk than a goat	
2.	Oral part of the face used for eating and smiling	
3.	Sounds that stretch *a*, *e*, *i*, *o* and *u* – elastic sounds	
4.	A group of houses and shops you can find on a map	
5.	Sir Isaac Newton named gravity and measured the force that has everything fall this direction	
6.	A standard unit of time with sixty minutes	
7.	The waves of vibration that ears detect and respond to	
8.	Brightly-colored plants that grow in people's gardens	
9.	A tiny mammal with a long tail that squeaks and eats cheese	
10.	Instantly! Right this minute. The present time.	
11.	The common or proper grammar term for a person, place or thing	
12.	A single family dwelling where people live	
13.	In a range like the Rockies or the Andes, it's a very high snow-capped point of sharp rock	
14.	The direction North American birds fly after summer	

nouns	sounds	mouse	mouth
mountain	vowels	town	down
cow	flowers	hour	house
south	now		

Brown /Aw/ – Advanced

What word with /Aw/ answers the statements below?

1.	Big white fluffy pillow of water vapour in the sky	
2.	Nocturnal bird of prey that is a symbol of wisdom	
3.	Woman's fancy button-up shirt made of fine material	
4.	Just not sure; an element of uncertainty	
5.	Built-in kitchen working surface for food preparation	
6.	Make information instantly known to a broad audience	
7.	Unit of volume or weight, there are 16 in a pound	
8.	Small streams of water forced upwards under pressure for public drinking or visual enjoyment	
9.	The edge of a property or defined area	
10.	Silly, colourful acrobatic circus entertainer	
11.	Bank service for safekeeping of personal or corporate finances	
12.	Facial expression of a smile turned upside down	
13.	Enunciate, the manner and articulation of speech	
14.	*Mille* in French; the number is ten times one hundred	

counter	frown	cloud	pronounce
thousand	clown	doubt	boundary
announce	fountain	account	ounce
owl	blouse		

Purple /ɛr/ – Basic

What word with /ɛr/ answers the statements below?

1.	Female child, or a daughter as in, *We have three boys and a _ _ _ _.*	
2.	Medical professional who gives needles and helps doctors	
3.	The shape that is round and flat like a coin or a ring	
4.	I starts with **v** and is the action part of a sentence	
5.	Woman's clothing accessory that is both fashionable and practical for carrying money and tissue	
6.	Our home planet, third from the sun in our solar system	
7.	An individual, either male or female, but only one of them	
8.	The most bad, awful day or experience	
9.	Clothing worn by males and females that covers the upper body that can have long or short sleeves	
10.	Big stuffed bird served with cranberries at Thanksgiving	
11.	Pronoun that indicates something belongs to a female	
12.	With cake, balloons and presents, friends celebrate this day you were born.	
13.	Fixed group of letters that is part of the vocabulary of a language	
14.	Past tense of *hear* that looks like *beard* and sounds like *bird*	

nurse	word	person	girl
heard	her	earth	circle
birthday	worst	verb	turkey
purse	shirt		

Chapter Two — Mystery Word Match — Vowels

Purple /Er/ – Advanced

What word with /Er/ answers the statements below?

1.	A policy purchased before a trip to pay for unexpected mechanical repairs and medical bills	
2.	Continent north of Africa on the eastern coast of the Atlantic Ocean	
3.	Drapery to adorn a window or shut out light completely	
4.	How many eggs in two and a half dozen?	
5.	Internet activity, browsing or randomly seeking out information	
6.	Laundry powder added to the washing machine to make dirty clothes clean	
7.	Collective noun for a large group of horses, cows or buffalo, etc.	
8.	All and everything the environment, all countries and all people	
9.	Irregular past participle of that crazy old verb *to be*	
10.	A long trip, either physically towards a destination or metaphorically through life	
11.	Recurring celebration on the date of a marriage or other special event	
12.	Worry or concern about a stressful situation, for example, *Public speaking makes me* _ _ _ _ _ _ _ _.	
13.	**R** on the gear-stick of an automatic car that stands for going backwards	
14.	It takes this to speak English out loud. The lion was looking for it in the Wizard of Oz.	

herd	nervous	thirty	journey
courage	Europe	were	insurance
curtain	anniversary	world	surfing
reverse	detergent		

Chapter Two — Mystery Word Match — Vowels

Charcoal /ʌr/ – Basic

What word with /ʌr/ answers the statements below?

1.	A synonym for difficult; the opposite of easy or soft	
2.	Internal organ that pumps blood, it's a symbol of Valentine's Day.	
3.	The grassy area outside the home where children play	
4.	Piece of clothing worn around the neck for warmth or fashion	
5.	The third month of the year; the solstice; when spring arrives	
6.	Uniformed protectors of the bank or the queen	
7.	Parts of the body needed for giving hugs	
8.	The size of big, baggy, casual comfortable clothing	
9.	Someone who lives in the country and works in the fields growing crops and vegetables	
10.	Once a week these smelly bags are picked up from the end of driveways.	
11.	Folded paper with special messages given on birthdays	
12.	The beginning and the end of *red car*	
13.	A place to buy fresh fruit and vegetables	
14.	Word for the beginning of a game or a race	

large	hard	start	farmer
guards	March	garbage	yard
heart	r	arms	market
scarf	cards		

Chapter Two — Mystery Word Match — Vowels

Charcoal /Ar/ – Advanced

What word with /Ar/ answers the statements below?

1.	A small blade in a cylindrical hole used to shave a point on a pencil	
2.	Pay for merchandise with a credit card instead of cash	
3.	Heated discussion, raised voices, differences of opinion involving	
4.	Non-commissioned US military officer above corporal	
5.	Deep pile wall-to-wall synthetic fabric floor covering	
6.	An individual who is legally responsible to care for another person physically and financially	
7.	Items purchased and sold at a greatly reduced price, often found at garage sales	
8.	The standard inch of white space on all sides of a printed document	
9.	The name of the prince who woke Sleeping Beauty with a kiss	
10.	Any oriental self-defence disciplines, such as karate, judo, or tae kwon do, usually practiced as sport	
11.	The relationship between people in business or marriage	
12.	Six-stringed musical instrument central to a rock band	
13.	Section of the airport dedicated to passengers leaving the area	
14.	Cardboard container for milk, juice or eggs	

margin	partner	guardian	departure
carpet	charge	charming	sharpener
martial arts	bargain	argument	guitar
carton	sergeant		

Orange /or/ – Basic

What word with /or/ answers the statements below?

1.	First part of the day, the time before 12 o'clock noon	
2.	Pants higher than the knee, worn in warm weather	
3.	Indoor walking surface made of linoleum, hardwood, tile or carpet	
4.	Long yellow vegetable that grows in fields on cobs	
5.	Body parts including heart, lungs, liver, brain and skin	
6.	The perfect temperature for springtime, fresh rolls and apple pie	
7.	Standard equipment at the front of the classroom where the teacher writes notes for students to read	
8.	Bad weather with heavy rain, lightening, thunder and high winds	
9.	Large farm animals suitable for riding or pulling wagons	
10.	Special feeling or quality that raises an event or person above others	
11.	To inform others of danger with a siren or sign	
12.	After third in an ordinal list; the last one needed for a square dance or game of bridge	
13.	Tale told to children that begins, *Once upon a time...*	
14.	Flatware with three or four sharp points for piercing food	

corn	organs	floor	storm
shorts	horse	board	important
morning	fourth	fork	warn
warm	story		

Chapter Two — Mystery Word Match — Vowels

Orange /Or/ – Advanced

What word with /Or/ answers the statements below?

1.	Holiday destination with spa, sports and relaxation	
2.	Specialized farm where fruit trees grow in tidy rows	
3.	Sad, painful, expensive, legal dissolution of a marriage	
4.	Open pit mine where heavy equipment loads sand and aggregate into trucks	
5.	Froggy voice early in the morning or caused by a sore throat	
6.	Boutique that sells and delivers flower arrangements, houseplants and gifts	
7.	Small treatable unsightly lumps on fingers and hands caused by virus	
8.	Lucky circumstances or positive turn of events	
9.	Woodwinds, strings, brass, percussion sections, etc., making a professional group of classical musicians	
10.	Goods and services exit the country and feature in the gross national product	
11.	Spongy beige plug that seals an expensive bottle of wine	
12.	Severe weather condition also known as a twister	
13.	Part of a desk or dresser that pulls open to reveal a shallow storage bin	
14.	The lion speaks tonight – what sound does he make?	

orchard	cork	divorce	fortunate
warts	quarry	florist	drawer
export	orchestra	resort	tornado
roar	hoarse		

Vowel Sound Maze

Instructions

Enter the maze at the ⬇ in the top left corner.

Connect the words that <u>contain</u> the sound indicated in the title of the worksheet, i.e. **/Ay/**.

Do not lift your pen from the page.

Do not cross over a solid line – only go through gaps in the lines on each side, top or bottom of the word square.

Exit the maze at the ⬇ using the shortest route possible.

Teacher note: For lower levels have the students complete the exercise in a group. It is helpful if they read the words out loud to each other.

Higher levels can determine the color of every word in each exercise.

(Solutions begin on page 227.)

 Animal Crackers

Why did the pony eat cough drops?

                                    He was a little hoarse.

What do bees do with their honey?

                                    They cell it.

What do you call a scared tyrannosaurus?

                                    A nervous rex.

What happens when frogs park illegally?

                                    They get toad.

What animal should you never play cards with?

                                    A cheetah.

Chapter Two — Mystery Maze — Vowels

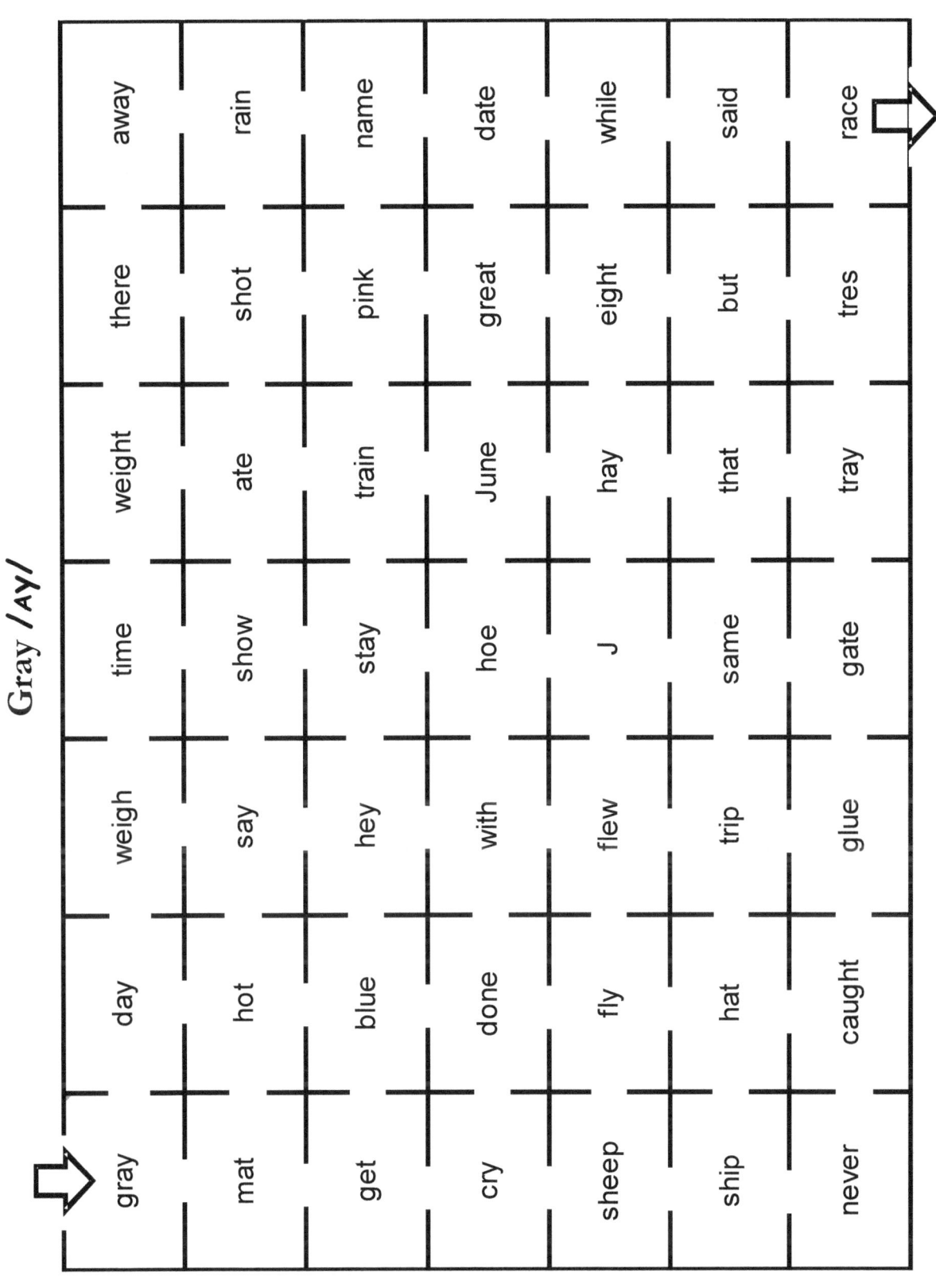

Gray /ʌɪ/

Chapter Two — Mystery Maze — Vowels

Red /e/

thing	store	juice	scene	west	guest	parent
other	the	guest	ocean	L	try	stretch
debt	from	father	pour	penny	stretch	exit
drop	next	many	vest	noise	gain	health
basket	get	cake	guess	five	nephew	N
tree	said	rice	very	motor	smell	taste
red	head	meat	friend	bread	any	ring

166

Chapter Two — Mystery Maze — Vowels

White /Iy/

prison	history	twist	sing	sky	hymn	pie →
bill	hide	why	find	ski	hill	style
his	cycle	weight	ride	quiet	women	wife
kiss	my	prize	is	knife	mix	height
little	myth	side	mist	right	eye	fly
fight	bite	sight	with	listen	wrist	Christ
→ white	pickle	sister	whistle	it	bride	in

Chapter Two Mystery Maze Vowels

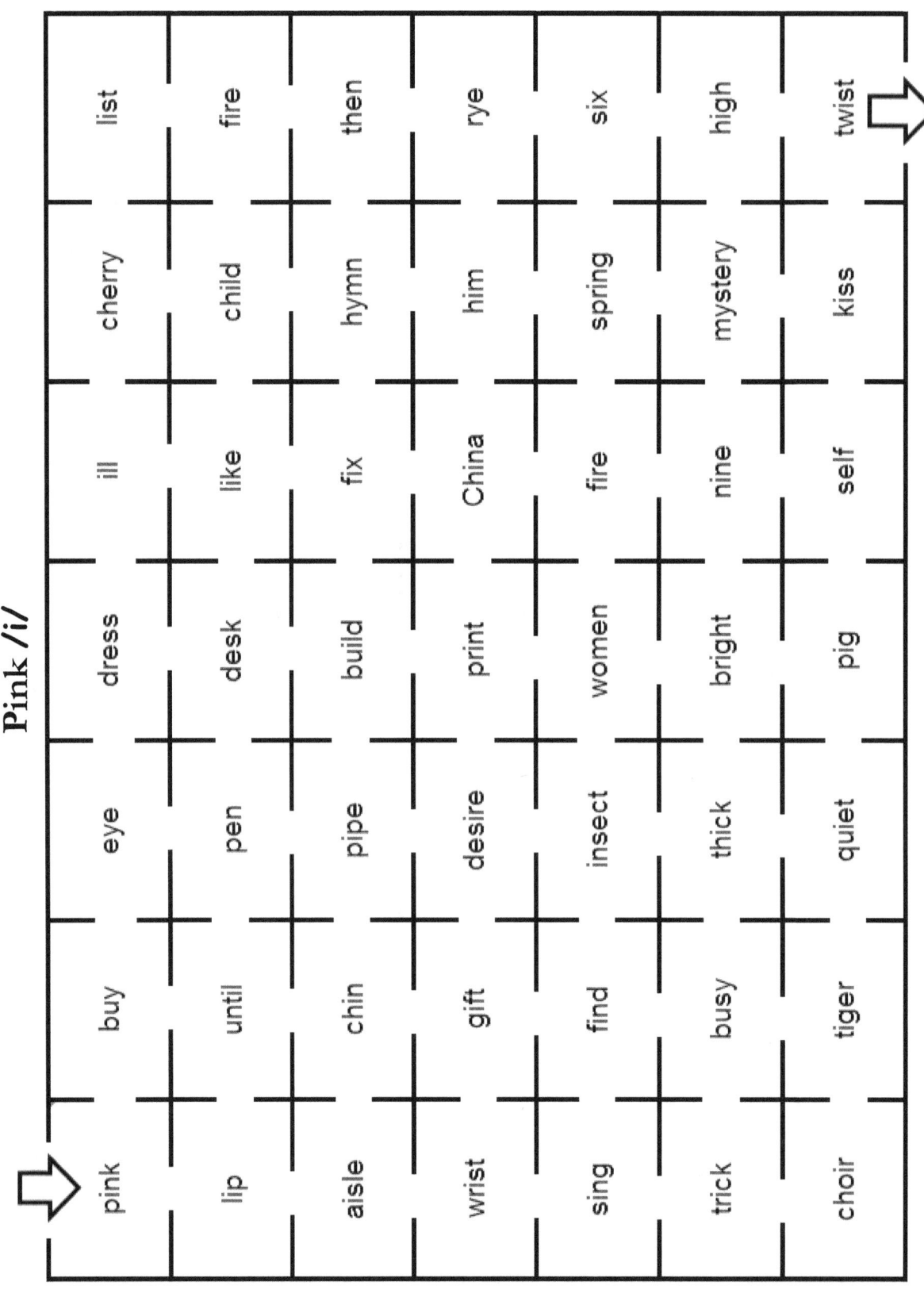

Pink /i/

list	fire	then	rye	six	high	twist →
cherry	child	hymn	him	spring	mystery	kiss
ill	like	fix	China	fire	nine	self
dress	desk	build	print	women	bright	pig
eye	pen	pipe	desire	insect	thick	quiet
buy	until	chin	gift	find	busy	tiger
→ pink	lip	aisle	wrist	sing	trick	choir

Chapter Two — Mystery Maze — Vowels

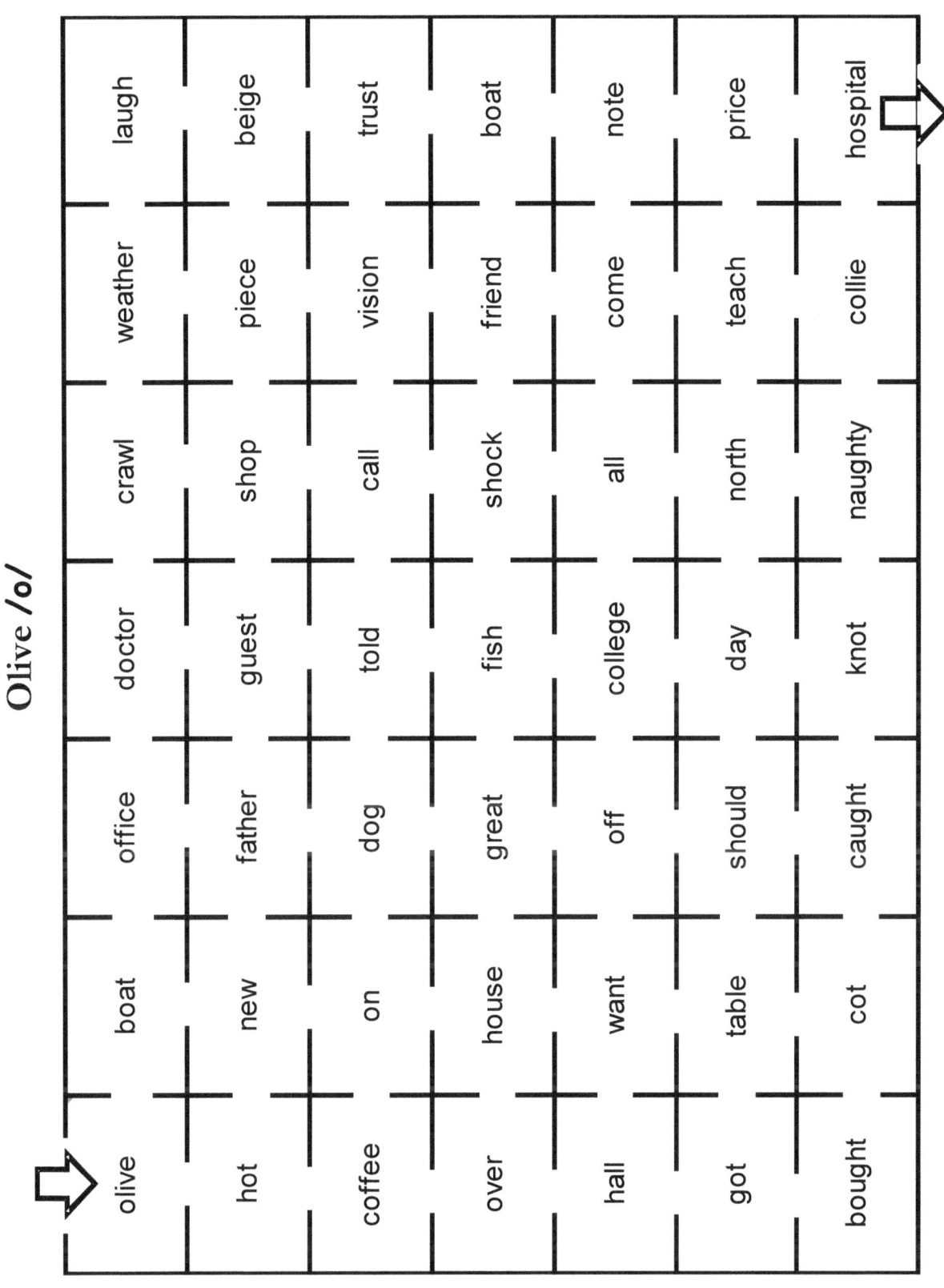

Telephone Alphabet Bingo

Blue /Uw/

blue	shoe	joke	bring	level	fly	drop
shut	cool	new	wish	sew	floor	play
come	ounce	who	jet	jewel	boot	due
open	juice	you	no	flute	change	soup
knew	tooth	love	to	moo	swing	music
suit	joint	shot	dew	cost	call	fool
glue	youth	beautiful	two	take	from	queue

Chapter Two　　　Mystery Maze　　　Vowels

Mustard /u/

zoo	does	done	come	cousin	south	love →
stood	rough	tuna	hook	stomach	money	was
pull	funny	country	hundred	Peru	look	pudding
put	loose	pool	the	human	kangaroo	cool
uniform	vowel	tongue	must	goose	nook	fruit
mother	from	public	cute	mustard	allow	due
→ mustard	blue	juice	look	balloon	amuse	noon

Chapter Two — Mystery Maze — Vowels

Brown /Aw/

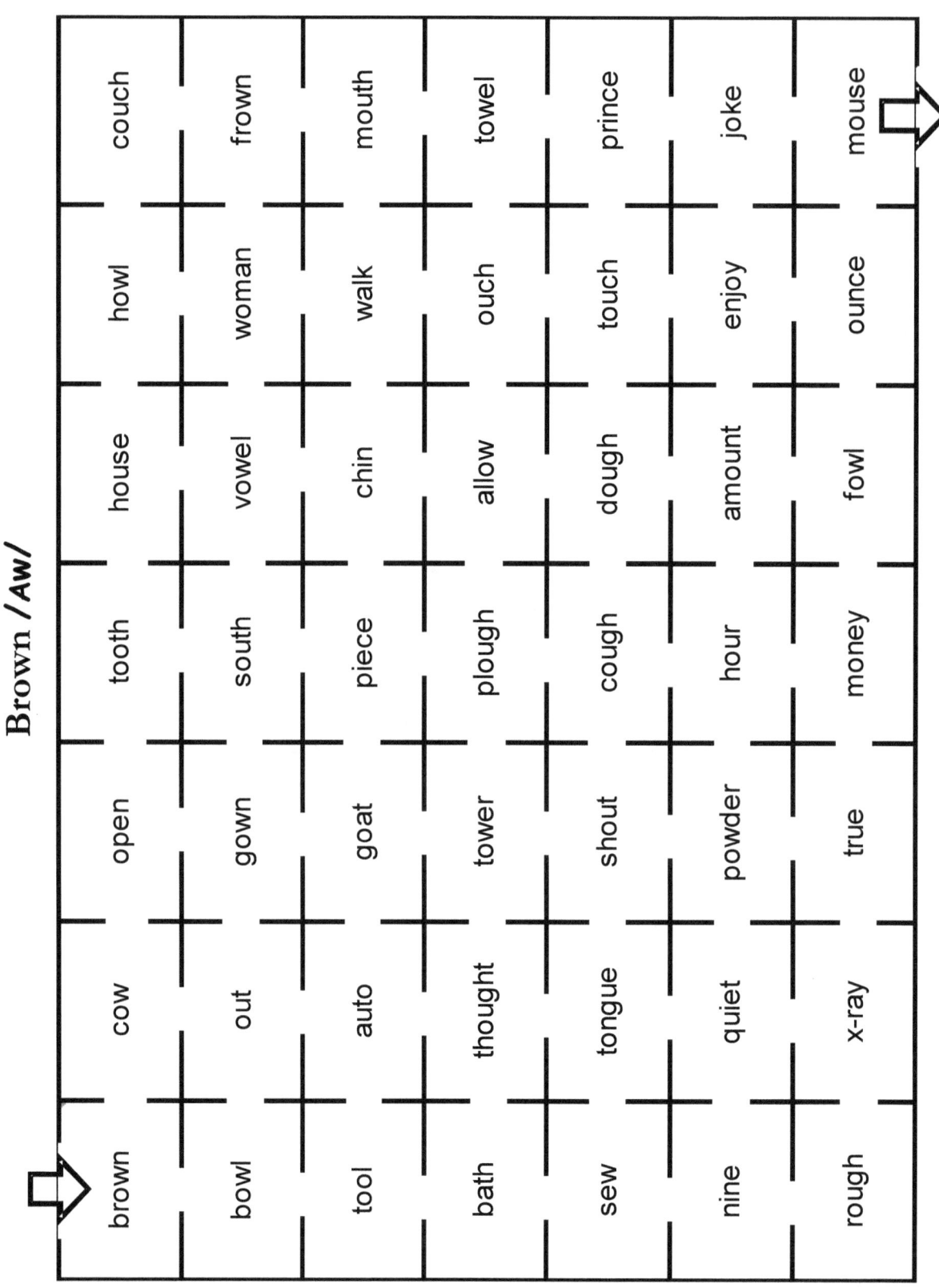

brown	cow	open	tooth	house	howl	couch
bowl	out	gown	south	vowel	woman	frown
tool	auto	goat	piece	chin	walk	mouth
bath	thought	tower	plough	allow	ouch	towel
sew	tongue	shout	cough	dough	touch	prince
nine	quiet	powder	hour	amount	enjoy	joke
rough	x-ray	true	money	fowl	ounce	mouse

→ start at "brown", exit at "mouse"

Chapter Two — Mystery Maze — Vowels

Purple /Er/

cord	star	fur	serve	third	skirt	burst →
arm	shirt	turtle	course	friend	jar	more
score	her	part	curtain	were	first	orange
mark	earn	certain	church	drawer	earth	four
dark	organ	artery	horn	jerk	bird	yard
herd	girl	nurse	barn	world	pork	torn
→ purple	farm	birth	work	alert	normal	resort

© Judy Thompson 2011 — www.ThompsonLanguageCenter.com

Domino Instructions

This game is a bit tricky to learn, but I like it.

Beginner students can work in groups of three or four. Intermediate students in pairs and advanced students on their own.

Photocopy a Domino sheet for every member of your class, but don't give it to them to them until the end of class. (They all want to take one home.)

Give a set of Dominos to each group or pair of students in the class.

The idea is to have them butt together words and build a track until all the pieces are used.

Lowest level:
>Any word can butt up to another word with the same sound color. **this** and **give** are both *pink* so they can butt together.

More difficult:
>Black has to butt with black and white has to butt with white.

More difficult:
>All the game pieces have to be connected in a giant sprawling unit.

More difficult still:
>All the game pieces have to complete a circuit.

Most difficult:
>All the pieces have to complete a circuit, black to black and white to white.

Hint: Have the partners say the words out loud to each other.

Use the activity two days in a row. The first day will be very slow. The second day will be much faster, and you can increase the difficulty level according to the guidelines above.

To be very nasty, time them or race groups against each other. The higher the level, the more restrictions there should be.

Dominos /Ay/ to /o/
Gray, Black, Green, Red, White, Pink, Yellow, Olive

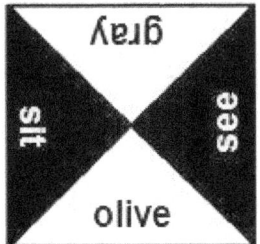
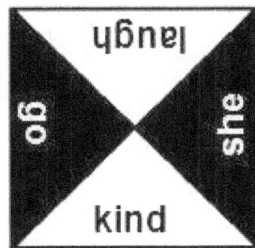

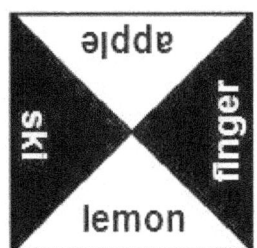

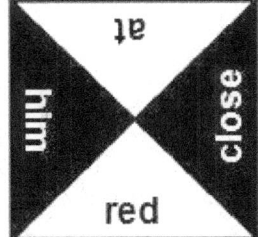

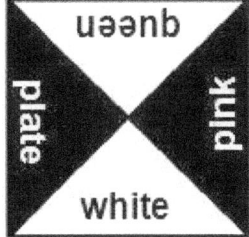

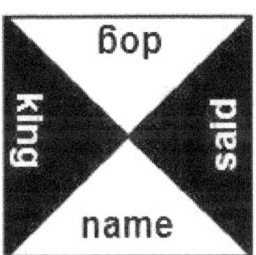

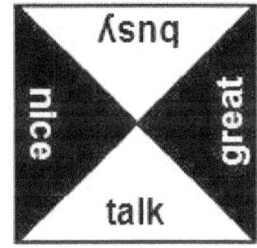

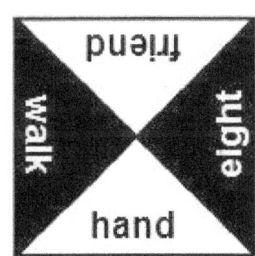
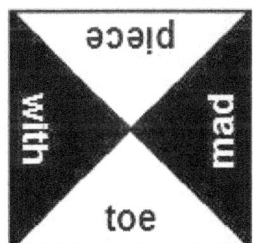
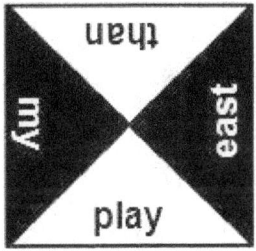

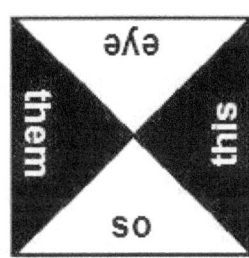
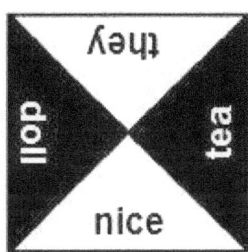

Dominos /Uw/ to /Or/
Blue, Mustard, Wood, Turquoise, Brown, Purple, Charcoal, Orange

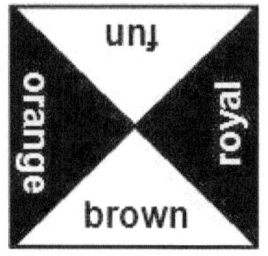

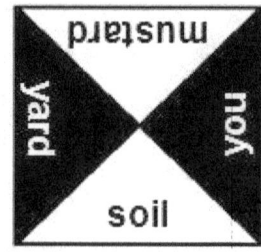

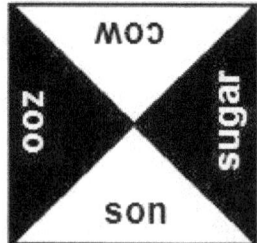
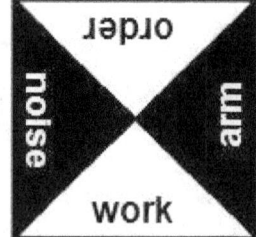

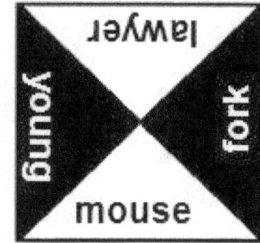

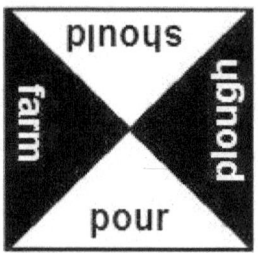
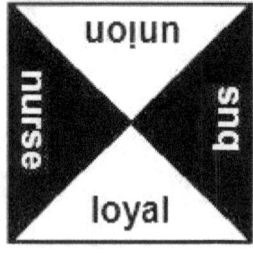

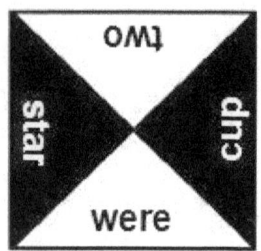
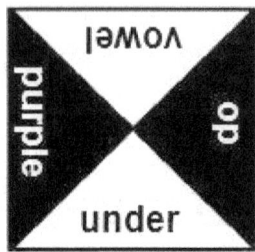

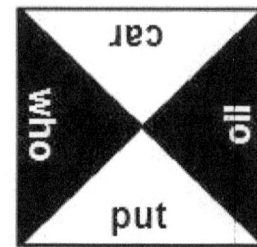
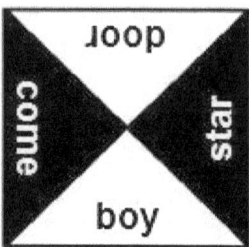
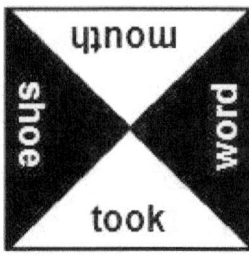

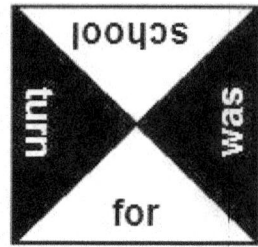
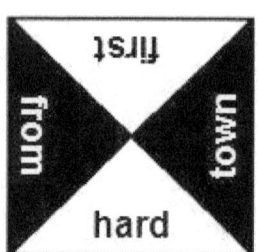

Bingo Rules

Look for the rules on pages 24 and 99.

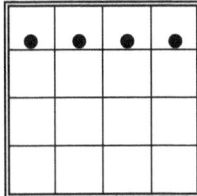 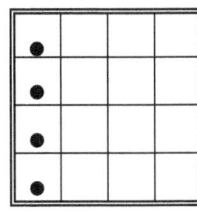 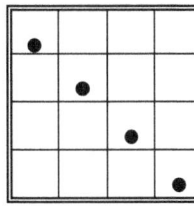 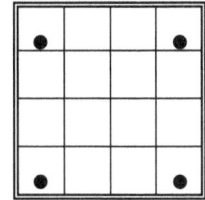

Bingo can be a type of game, a clapping song or a stand-alone expression of assent. Bingo is part of North American culture.

The Bingo Song
I remember Farmer Brown, he had a dog, and Bingo was his name oh...
… apparently these are no longer the words. Now they teach:

There was a farmer, had a dog and Bingo was his name – o
B-I-N-G-O, B-I-N-G-O, B-I-N-G-O, and BINGO was his name-o

There was a farmer, had a dog and Bingo was his name – o
(clap)-I-N-G-O, (clap) –I-N-G-O, (clap)-I-N-G-O, and BINGO was his name-o

There was a farmer, had a dog and Bingo was his name – o
(clap – clap)-N-G-O, (clap – clap)-N-G-O, (clap – clap)-N-G-O, and BINGO was his name-o …

Look at 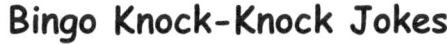http://www.youtube.com/watch?v=KUDZiu_SVzw

Bingo Knock-Knock Jokes

Knock! Knock !
   Who's there?
Bingo !
   Bingo who?
Bingo'ng to come and see you for ages !

Knock! Knock!

   Who's there?
Bee Eye.
   Bee Eye who?
B-I-N-G-O, B-I-N-G-O, B-I-N-G-O, and BINGO is my name-o

Vowel Bingo Word List

mail	square
grass	salad
cream	field
next	ready
child	height
which	pretty
shoulder	whole
August	coffee
cube	juice
jungle	from
cookie	woman
coin	toilet
round	down
turn	person
dark	heart
fourth	border

Chapter Two — Vowel Bingo — Vowels

Card 1

/Or/	/Uw/	/Ey/	/Ay/
/Ar/	/u/	/Er/	/i/
/o/	/Aw/	/Iy/	/^/
/e/	/Oy/	/Ow/	/a/

Card 2

/Ay/	/a/	/Ar/	/Or/
/Ey/	/Aw/	/Er/	/e/
/i/	/Iy/	/^/	/Oy/
/Ow/	/u/	/o/	/Uw/

Card 3

/u/	/Iy/	/Or/	/^/
/o/	/Er/	/Uw/	/a/
/e/	/Ow/	/Ar/	/Ey/
/Oy/	/Ay/	/i/	/Aw/

Card 4

/Ow/	/u/	/Ey/	/Er/
/Ar/	/e/	/a/	/Oy/
/Uw/	/Or/	/i/	/^/
/Iy/	/o/	/Ay/	/Aw/

How can you tell twin witches apart?
You can't always tell which witch is which.

Chapter Two Vowel Bingo Vowels

Card 5

/Uw/	/Ar/	/^/	/Ow/
/Aw/	/Iy/	/Or/	/e/
/a/	/o/	/Ey/	/i/
/Oy/	/Er/	/u/	/Ay/

Card 6

/e/	/Ar/	/a/	/o/
/Or/	/Uw/	/Ow/	/^/
/Aw/	/i/	/Er/	/u/
/Oy/	/Ay/	/Iy/	/Ey/

Card 7

/Ar/	/Oy/	/e/	/i/
/Er/	/^/	/Ow/	/Ay/
/Or/	/o/	/Uw/	/Iy/
/a/	/Ey/	/Aw/	/u/

Card 8

/i/	/Ow/	/Aw/	/o/
/Ey/	/a/	/Ar/	/Uw/
/Or/	/Iy/	/^/	/Er/
/u/	/Oy/	/e/	/Ay/

 How many months have 28 days?
All of them.

Chapter Two — Vowel Bingo — Vowels

Card 9

/Uw/	/a/	/Ey/	/Iy/
/Or/	/Oy/	/Ow/	/Er/
/Aw/	/i/	/u/	/Ar/
/o/	/e/	/Ay/	/^/

Card 10

/^/	/Ow/	/Er/	/a/
/Uw/	/e/	/Oy/	/i/
/Or/	/Ay/	/o/	/Ar/
/Iy/	/Aw/	/Ey/	/u/

Card 11

/Er/	/Ay/	/Uw/	/Or/
/Ar/	/o/	/Aw/	/Iy/
/u/	/Ey/	/i/	/^/
/a/	/Oy/	/Ow/	/e/

Card 12

/a/	/Uw/	/Aw/	/i/
/Er/	/u/	/Ey/	/Ar/
/Iy/	/^/	/e/	/Ay/
/i/	/Oy/	/Ow/	/Or/

Teacher: What is a pirate's favorite letter?
Ryan: Argh!
Teacher: He likes the *Argh!* But he loves the *Sea*.

Chapter Two — Vowel Bingo — Vowels

/ow/	/e/	/aw/	/Er/
/^/	/u/	/or/	/o/
/Iy/	/Uw/	/a/	/Ay/
/Ar/	/i/	/Ey/	/oy/

13

/Uw/	/Iy/	/^/	/i/
/Er/	/o/	/Ay/	/ow/
/Ey/	/Ar/	/oy/	/u/
/Aw/	/e/	/a/	/or/

14

/Er/	/o/	/Aw/	/i/
/oy/	/Iy/	/Ey/	/e/
/u/	/Ar/	/a/	/Uw/
/Ay/	/^/	/or/	/ow/

15

/Ey/	/Er/	/a/	/ow/
/Uw/	/o/	/Ar/	/^/
/Iy/	/e/	/i/	/Ay/
/oy/	/or/	/Aw/	/u/

16

Spider: Sorry I'm late. I was answering my email.
Ladybug: You get email? How?
Spider: Simple, I'm on the web.

Chapter Two — Vowel Bingo — Vowels

Card 17

/Oy/	/Ay/	/^/	/Ow/
/Iy/	/e/	/i/	/Er/
/Uw/	/Ar/	/Ey/	/a/
/Aw/	/o/	/Or/	/u/

Card 18

/i/	/e/	/Or/	/^/
/a/	/Uw/	/Ey/	/o/
/Aw/	/Er/	/Oy/	/u/
/Ow/	/Iy/	/Ar/	/Ay/

Card 19

/i/	/Iy/	/Ey/	/Aw/
/Ar/	/Oy/	/Or/	/a/
/Ow/	/Ay/	/o/	/Er/
/e/	/Uw/	/^/	/u/

Card 20

/Ey/	/i/	/Aw/	/Oy/
/Or/	/^/	/a/	/Er/
/Ay/	/e/	/o/	/Iy/
/Ar/	/Uw/	/u/	/Ow/

How did the geometry teacher grade her students?
Fair and square

Fun with Vowel Sounds

What is at the beginning of eternity,
the end of time and space,
the beginning of every end
and the end of every place?

The letter e

Part of North American Culture

Rhymes and songs are wonderful tools for learning the sounds, culture and history of a language. North Americans know this rhyme well but may not know it originated hundreds of years ago as a protest by English sheep farmers. The poor farmers were required to pay one-third of their income to the king (master), one-third to the church (dame) and only allowed to keep one-third of their produce for themselves (little boy who lived down the lane).

Baa Baa Black Sheep

Baa baa black sheep have you any wool?	/ba ba blak ShEyp hav yUw enEy w^l/
Yes sir, yes sir, three bags full.	/yes sEr yes sEr THrEy bagz f^l/
One for my master and one for my dame,	/wun fOr mIy mastEr an wun fOr mIy dAym/
One for the little boy who lives down the lane.	/wun fOr Thu lidel bOy hUw livz dAwn thu lAyn/
Baa baa black sheep have you any wool?	/ba ba blak ShEyp hav yUw enEy w^l/
Yes sir, yes sir, three bags full.	/yes sEr yes sEr THrEy bagz f^l/

Cry Wolf

Once upon a time, a lonely shepherd boy sat high in a mountain meadow watching his sheep. Nothing unusual ever happened on the quiet hillside so the boy decided to play a trick on the townspeople. He cried, *Wolf! Wolf! Wolf!* The villagers ran up the hill armed with sticks to drive the wolf away. There was no wolf.

Everyone was angry that the boy was just pulling their leg, but the boy enjoyed his little joke. The next day he cried, *Wolf! Wolf! The wolf is eating the sheep!* Again the villagers ran to help. The boy laughed at them.

On the third day, a big hungry wolf attacked the sheep. The terrified boy screamed for help, but no one came. The wolf ate all the sheep. The boy realized too late the importance of telling the truth.

Sound Search – Vowels

Search the story for examples of vowel sounds. Put one or two examples beside each EPA sound symbol. (Solution is on page 227.)

/Ay/	play	/Uw/	
/a/		/u/	
/Ey/		/^/	
/e/		/Oy/	
/Iy/		/Aw/	
/i/		/Er/	
/Ow/		/Ar/	
/o/		/Or/	

What do sheep sing on their birthdays?
Happy Birthday to ewe.

Chapter Three

TRANSCRIPTIONS

A different language is a different vision of life.
Federico Fellini

Line Match – Basic

Match the phonetic words in the first column to their spellings in the second. The first one is done for you. (Solution is on page 228.)

/nIyn/	nose
/pErpel/	turkey
/grEyn/	cheese
/hed/	nine
/nOz/	fruit
/ChEyk/	purple
/nAyl/	circle
/nukel/	talk
/pom/	cheek
/tErkEy/	knee
/mEyt/	green
/frUwt/	palm
/ChEyz/	tooth
/apel/	nail
/sErkel/	apple
/skwAyr/	meat
/tok/	lion
/tUwTH/	knuckle
/nEy/	head
/lIyon/	square

 **What happened to the plant on the windowsill of the math classroom?**
It grew square roots.

Line Match – Advanced

Match the phonetic words in the first column to their spellings in the second. The first one is done for you. (Solution is on page 228.)

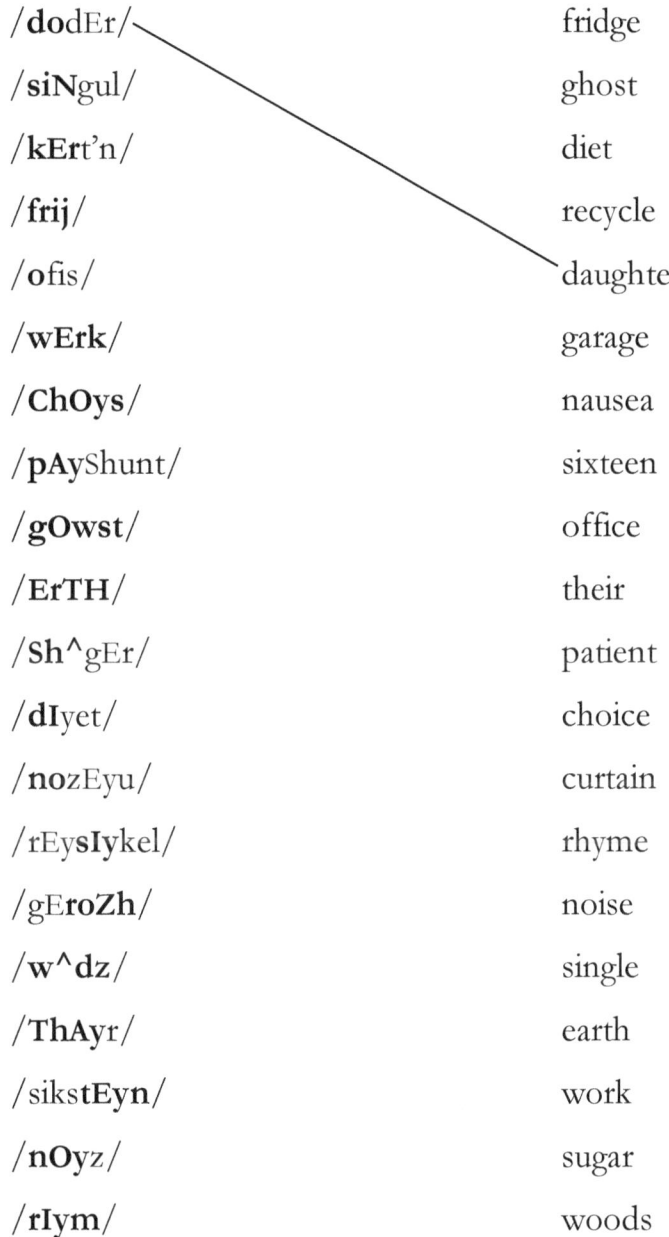

/**do**dEr/ — daughter
/**siN**gul/
/**kEr**t'n/
/**frij**/
/**o**fis/
/**wEr**k/
/**ChOy**s/
/**pAy**Shunt/
/**gOw**st/
/**Er**TH/
/**Sh^**gEr/
/**dI**yet/
/**no**zEyu/
/**rEy**sIykel/
/**gE**roZh/
/**w^**dz/
/**ThAy**r/
/**siks**tEyn/
/**nOy**z/
/**rIy**m/

fridge
ghost
diet
recycle
daughter
garage
nausea
sixteen
office
their
patient
choice
curtain
rhyme
noise
single
earth
work
sugar
woods

Patient: Nurse, the doctor was here and used a four-letter word that upset me.
Nurse: What did he say?
Patient: Oops!

Transcription Treats

/fUwd/ f o o d – Basic

Transcribe the following words from *spoken English* (EPA) to written English. The first one is done for you. (Solution is on page 228.)

/kArut/	<u>c a r r o t</u>	/jUws/	_ _ _ _ _
/bred/	_ _ _ _ _	/sosej/	_ _ _ _ _ _
/selErEy/	_ _ _ _ _ _	/zUwkEynEy/	_ _ _ _ _ _ _ _
/putAydu/	_ _ _ _ _ _	/Sh^gEr/	_ _ _ _ _
/kUwkumbEr/	_ _ _ _ _ _ _ _	/wEyt/	_ _ _ _ _
/striNg bEyn/	_ _ _ _ _ _ _ _ _ _	/CherEyz/	_ _ _ _ _ _ _ _
/unyun/	_ _ _ _ _	/pEyChiz/	_ _ _ _ _ _
/gArlik/	_ _ _ _ _ _	/Orunjiz/	_ _ _ _ _ _ _
/kofEy/	_ _ _ _ _ _	/rAyzunz/	_ _ _ _ _ _
/ChEyz/	_ _ _ _ _ _	/dAyts/	_ _ _ _ _
/budEr/	_ _ _ _ _ _	/ledus/	_ _ _ _ _ _ _
/Chikun THIyz/	_ _ _ _ _ _ _ _ _ _ _ _ _	/bEyf Ow ZhUw/	_ _ _ _ _ _ _ _ _

Why did the donut shop close?
The owner got tired of the (w)hole business.

/klOwz/ c l o t h e s – Basic

Transcribe the following words from *spoken English* (EPA) to written English. The first one is done for you. (Solution is on page 228.)

/ShErt/	<u>s h i r t</u>	/wolet/	_ _ _ _ _ _
/swedEr/	_ _ _ _ _ _ _	/gAwn/	_ _ _ _
/jEynz/	_ _ _ _ _	/yUwnifOrm/	_ _ _ _ _ _ _
/sUwt/	_ _ _ _	/dres/	_ _ _ _ _
/tIy/	_ _ _	/ShOrts/	_ _ _ _
/gluvz/	_ _ _ _ _ _	/pErs/	_ _ _ _ _
/woCh/	_ _ _ _ _	/skArf/	_ _ _ _ _
/blAwz/	_ _ _ _ _ _	/jakut/	_ _ _ _ _ _
/rAynkOwt/	_ _ _ _ _ _ _ _	/EyriNgz/	_ _ _ _ _ _ _ _
/loNg jonz/	_ _ _ _ _ _ _ _	/bUwts/	_ _ _ _ _
/goChEyz/	_ _ _ _ _ _ _ _	/glasiz/	_ _ _ _ _ _ _
/soks/	_ _ _ _ _	/brAyslet/	_ _ _ _ _ _ _ _

Where do fashionable ghosts shop for clothes?
Boo-tiques

Chapter Three   Transcriptions Treats   Transcriptions

/bodEy/ b o d y – Basic

Transcribe the following words from *spoken English* (EPA) to written English. The first one is done for you. (Solution is on page 228.)

/hed/	h e a d	/hAyr/	_ _ _ _
/Iy/	_ _ _	/ThrOwt/	_ _ _ _ _ _
/nOwz/	_ _ _ _	/tuNg/	_ _ _ _ _ _
/tEyTH/	_ _ _ _ _	/tumEy/	_ _ _ _ _
/f^t/	_ _ _ _	/rist/	_ _ _ _ _
/mAwTH/	_ _ _ _ _	/luNgz/	_ _ _ _ _
/nEyz/	_ _ _ _ _	/hArt/	_ _ _ _ _
/fiNgEr/	_ _ _ _ _ _	/stumuk/	_ _ _ _ _ _ _
/pom/	_ _ _ _	/Iybrow/	_ _ _ _ _ _ _
/nukul/	_ _ _ _ _ _ _	/frekul/	_ _ _ _ _ _ _
/nAylz/	_ _ _ _ _	/fOrArm/	_ _ _ _ _ _ _
/musul/	_ _ _ _ _ _	/Eyrz/	_ _ _ _

 What is the best thing to put into a pie?
Your teeth

Chapter Three /numbErz and komun wErdz/
numbers and common words

Transcribe the following words from *spoken English* (EPA) to written English. The first one is done for you. (Solution is on page 228.)

/wun/	o n e	/iz/	_ _
/tUw/	_ _ _	/wuz/	_ _ _
/THrEy/	_ _ _ _ _	/duz/	_ _ _ _
/fIyv/	_ _ _ _	/Thu/	_ _ _
/siks/	_ _ _	/wok/	_ _ _ _
/Ayt/	_ _ _ _ _	/laf/	_ _ _ _ _
/twenEy/	_ _ _ _ _ _	/frum/	_ _ _ _
/THErdEy/	_ _ _ _ _ _	/wEy/	_ _
/fOrdEy/	_ _ _ _ _	/ThAy/	_ _ _ _
/sevenEy/	_ _ _ _ _ _ _	/uv/	_ _
/hundrEd/	_ _ _ _ _ _ _	/cof/	_ _ _ _ _
/THAwzund/	_ _ _ _ _ _ _ _	/lidul/	_ _ _ _ _ _

Why is 6 afraid of 7?
Because 7, 8, 9

/skUwl wErdz/ s c h o o l w o r d s

Transcribe the following words from *spoken English* (EPA) to written English. The first one is done for you. (Solution is on page 228.)

/klas/	c l a s s	/lisen/	_ _ _ _ _ _
/tEyChEr/	_ _ _ _ _ _ _	/kwesjun/	_ _ _ _ _ _ _ _
/stUwdunt/	_ _ _ _ _ _ _	/ansEr/	_ _ _ _ _ _
/perent/	_ _ _ _ _ _	/rEyd/	_ _ _ _
/pAypEr/	_ _ _ _ _	/rIyt/	_ _ _ _ _
/wErk/	_ _ _ _	/alfubet/	_ _ _ _ _ _ _ _
/iNgliSh/	_ _ _ _ _ _ _	/Ay/	_
/ofis/	_ _ _ _ _ _	/bEy/	_
/kumpUwder/	_ _ _ _ _ _ _ _ _	/sEy/	_
/kwIyet/	_ _ _ _ _	/AyCh/	_
/skrEyn/	_ _ _ _ _ _	/kyUw/	_
/ChAyr/	_ _ _ _ _	/sukses/	_ _ _ _ _ _ _

Why did the Cyclops have to shut down his school?
He had only one pupil.

/envIyErment/ e n v i r o n m e n t – Advanced

Transcribe the following words from *spoken English* (EPA) to written English. The first one is done for you. (Solution is on page 228.)

EPA	Word	EPA	Word
/trEyz/	<u>t r e e s</u>	/prOwtekShun/	_____
/bErdz/	_____	/EyrowZhun/	_____
/nAyChEr/	_____	/rEyUwz/	_____
/sOwlEr/	_____	/EyfiShunsEy/	_____
/enErjEy/	_____	/consErv/	_____
/pulUwShun/	_____	/oltErnudiv/	_____
/gArbuj/	_____	/THEr mul/	_____
/rEysIykel/	_____	/bIyOwfUwel/	_____
/kompOwst/	_____	/nuklEyEr/	_____
/hIydrOw/	_____	/pAwEr/	_____
/pOyzun/	_____	/bIyOwsfEyr/	_____
/insulAyt/	_____	/spEysEyz/	_____

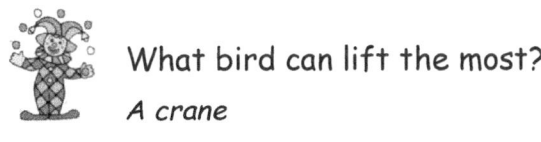

What bird can lift the most?

A crane

Chapter Three Transcriptions Treats Transcriptions

/medikul/ m e d i c a l – Advanced

Transcribe the following words from *spoken English* (EPA) to written English. The first one is done for you. (Solution is on page 229.)

/**al**Erj**E**y/	<u>a l l e r g y</u>	/**sEr**jun/	_ _ _ _ _ _ _
/**Th**erap**E**y/	_ _ _ _ _ _ _	/d**I**y**e**ti**S**hun/	_ _ _ _ _ _ _ _
/**vi**Zhun/	_ _ _ _ _ _	/pera**me**dik/	_ _ _ _ _ _ _ _
/**kon**Shus/	_ _ _ _ _ _ _ _ _	/**me**disun/	_ _ _ _ _ _ _ _
/**sti**Chiz/	_ _ _ _ _ _ _	/**pAy**Shunt/	_ _ _ _ _ _ _
/d**I**ya**be**dik/	_ _ _ _ _ _ _ _	/h**I**y**je**nist/	_ _ _ _ _ _ _ _ _
/**bun**Iyn/	_ _ _ _ _ _	/**ka**vid**E**y/	_ _ _ _ _ _
/**ste**THuskOwp/	_ _ _ _ _ _ _ _ _ _ _	/ap**Oyn**tmunt/	_ _ _ _ _ _ _ _ _ _ _
/**srinj**/	_ _ _ _ _ _ _	/**hel**THEy/	_ _ _ _ _ _ _
/pr**Ow**s**Ey**jEr/	_ _ _ _ _ _ _ _	/op**E**r**Ay**Shun/	_ _ _ _ _ _ _ _ _
/**ho**sbidul/	_ _ _ _ _ _ _ _	/**kli**nik/	_ _ _ _ _ _
/ku**les**tErol/	_ _ _ _ _ _ _ _ _ _ _	/**fi**zikul/	_ _ _ _ _ _ _ _

 How did the ESL student get to the hospital?
By accident

Chapter Three Transcriptions Treats Transcriptions

/wErkplAys/ w o r k p l a c e – Advanced

Transcribe the following words from *spoken English* (EPA) to written English. The first one is done for you. (Solution is on page 229.)

EPA	English	EPA	English
/kontrakt/	<u>c o n t r a c t</u>	/sekyEridEy/	_ _ _ _ _ _ _
/wAyjiz/	_ _ _ _ _	/ofis/	_ _ _ _ _ _
/pAyrOwl/	_ _ _ _ _ _	/opErAydEr/	_ _ _ _ _ _ _ _
/dEydukShun/	_ _ _ _ _ _ _ _ _	/rEykrUwdEr/	_ _ _ _ _ _ _ _
/prumOwShun/	_ _ _ _ _ _ _ _ _	/intErvUw/	_ _ _ _ _ _ _ _ _
/clIyent/	_ _ _ _ _ _	/netwErk/	_ _ _ _ _ _ _
/enjinEyr/	_ _ _ _ _ _ _ _	/rezUwmAy/	_ _ _ _ _ _
/dEyzIynEr/	_ _ _ _ _ _ _ _	/opShunz/	_ _ _ _ _ _ _
/sErvis/	_ _ _ _ _ _ _	/prOwbAyShun/	_ _ _ _ _ _ _ _ _
/Eylektronik/	_ _ _ _ _ _ _ _ _	/voluntEyr/	_ _ _ _ _ _ _ _ _
/mekanik/	_ _ _ _ _ _ _ _	/lAybErOr/	_ _ _ _ _ _ _
/faktEry/	_ _ _ _ _ _ _	/wader-kUwlEr/	_ _ _ _ _ _ - _ _ _ _ _ _

 **How do you keep a snake from striking?**
Pay it decent wages.

Chapter Three   Transcriptions Treats   Transcriptions

Déjà Vu – Advanced

(Solution is on page 229.)

/gErl/ _ _ _ _   /Ardik/ _ _ _ _ _ _
/jIyent/ _ _ _ _ _   /plEyz/ _ _ _ _ _ _
/kof/ _ _ _ _ _   /Ayk/ _ _ _ _
/ChelOw/ _ _ _ _ _   /kwIyEr/ _ _ _ _ _
/ShugEr/ _ _ _ _ _   /dogz/ _ _ _ _
/yUwZhUwul/ _ _ _ _ _   /kats/ _ _ _ _
/nAyShun/ _ _ _ _ _ _   /wok/ _ _ _ _
/nAyChEr/ _ _ _ _ _ _   /egzit/ _ _ _ _
/ejukAyShun/ _ _ _ _ _ _ _ _ _   /febyUwerEy/ _ _ _ _ _ _ _ _
/kwesjun/ _ _ _ _ _ _ _ _   /senChErEy/ _ _ _ _ _ _ _
/ansEr/ _ _ _ _ _ _   /kampAyn/ _ _ _ _ _ _ _ _
/hUw/ _ _ _   /kwOrdEr/ _ _ _ _ _ _ _
/wen/ _ _ _ _   /siks/ _ _ _
/bErTHdAy/ _ _ _ _ _ _ _ _   /nOrTH/ _ _ _ _ _
/sIyn/ _ _ _ _   /lEyg/ _ _ _ _ _ _
/bizEy/ _ _ _ _   /pleZhEr/ _ _ _ _ _ _ _ _
/vEyikel/ _ _ _ _ _ _ _   /raket/ _ _ _ _ _ _
/nAymz/ _ _ _ _ _   /pEytzu/ _ _ _ _ _ _
/AyZhu/ _ _ _ _   /yUwnyun/ _ _ _ _ _
/siNg/ _ _ _ _   /onEr/ _ _ _ _ _
/OwShun/ _ _ _ _ _   /wiSht/ _ _ _ _ _ _
/haf/ _ _ _ _   /danst/ _ _ _ _ _ _
/antEyk/ _ _ _ _ _ _ _   /laft/ _ _ _ _ _ _ _
/krismus/ _ _ _ _ _ _ _ _ _   /ast/ _ _ _ _ _
/paShun/ _ _ _ _ _ _ _   /sOwShul/ _ _ _ _ _ _
/tOylet/ _ _ _ _ _ _   /bu'n/ _ _ _ _ _ _
/bufAy/ _ _ _ _ _ _   /yErup/ _ _ _ _ _ _
/Orunj/ _ _ _ _ _ _   /gEroZh/ _ _ _ _ _ _
/wut/ _ _ _ _   /bOwTH/ _ _ _ _

Double Trouble Word Search

Part One:
- Translate the EPA speaking symbols at the bottom of the page into their written words.

Part Two:
- Circle all the words hidden in the puzzle.
- The words can be printed in any direction – left to right, right to left, top to bottom, bottom to top, diagonally or backwards.

(Solutions start on page 229.)

The list at the bottom of the game shows all of the words that are hidden in the puzzle.

Easy Beginner Word Search

S	P	K	C	H	F	J	P	I	H	E	T	K	P	P
U	C	A	K	O	W	V	W	A	O	O	N	C	X	I
S	R	H	P	E	O	P	L	E	R	D	G	O	A	N
P	Y	Q	O	C	W	A	R	M	S	K	E	N	H	K
K	V	D	H	O	E	T	X	E	E	Y	S	E	J	P
Q	J	A	V	U	L	Y	P	P	A	H	U	S	A	E
S	I	R	L	S	R	R	J	W	R	Q	O	C	H	C
R	S	B	F	G	H	V	P	W	L	T	H	A	J	B

/bluw/ _ _ _ _   /worm/ _ _ _ _   /fown/ _ _ _ _ _
/hors/ _ _ _ _ _   /hapEy/ _ _ _ _ _   /piNgk/ _ _ _ _
/kAr/ _ _ _   /pArk/ _ _ _ _   /hAws/ _ _ _ _ _
/chAyr/ _ _ _ _   /pEypul/ _ _ _ _ _ _ /skuwl/ _ _ _ _ _ _

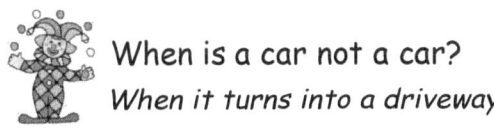

When is a car not a car?
When it turns into a driveway.

Chapter Three   Word Search   Transcriptions

/fUwd/ Food

```
C N R U F J P V E G E T A B L E S Q C R
O N Q V T E Z A K C U D A W T S P A E I
O I Q B A T E O S E I F H U H B B G T B
K S A L A M I B N T M E N T M B R P X S
I S N E K C I H C O A A R A A U C O R N
N E Z Z U P B D T M U L G B Q M P B Q
G I P U F Z M Z L H G L E M W W C J S O
V R H C C F I S D O E L A Z M A V R X L
Z E E S P C R I Y Z Y H E S A D I U F M
E C E M L A H K T C A U O A N I T F S Q
B O X V Y K S I G X U C X D G L A Q T P
B R H K C A S N N V N X X A O M C W Y J
Z G S U V W M T P I S M Z F P X E T A E
M A I I H M K H U F L H G I H T P A Y R
W E F Q P K V J R N S R V P E X M Z T M
```

/bEyf/ _ _ _ _   /kabaj/ _ _ _ _ _ _ _   /Chiken/ _ _ _ _ _ _ _
/k^kiNg/ _ _ _ _ _ _ _   /kOwrn/ _ _ _ _   /duk/ _ _ _ _
/fish/ _ _ _ _   /grOwsherEyz/ _ _ _ _ _ _ _ _   /hambErgEr/ _ _ _ _ _ _ _ _ _
/lam/ _ _ _ _   /mEyt/ _ _ _ _   /nuts/ _ _ _ _
/pastu/ _ _ _ _ _   /ribz/ _ _ _ _   /sulamEy/ _ _ _ _ _ _
/samon/ _ _ _ _ _ _   /Shrimp/ _ _ _ _ _ _   /THIy/ _ _ _ _ _
/maNgOw/ _ _ _ _ _   /tUwna/ _ _ _ _   /vejtubul/ _ _ _ _ _ _ _ _ _
/wEyt/ _ _ _ _ _   /yOwgErt/ _ _ _ _ _ _   /zUwkEynEy/ _ _ _ _ _ _ _ _

What does and invisible cat drink?
Evaporated milk

/klOwz/ Clothes

```
J C G S H I R T F E U B H G J G N T F J
E O N T R I K S O R X F S U L W O W T B
A L I C L H R W I D A H F O Z O T E I M
N L H C C A G K N V R C V T B O T R A Q
S A T U N I F O R M T E S S Y A U H B A
U R O H I R U T Z E T U S H O E B F T L
R H L C F T X S K T L S U S C X Q N D E
D A C D F U O C B J E P U F O G N B B I
Y H E I K M O Z V H B S C I A T T D L E
A V T W A P S D T T T Z W X T A H I S I
F O Z Z R E B O P F I E L E J K W U G P
Z Q I P N E L H Q E M Y K O A E E N Q X
V V L T S C D E V E E L S C A T Z R E M
S P I N J K S N A A H X F R A O E V G V
F P Y Z G D L C U Y B B H Q L J Q R R L
```

/belt/ _ _ _ _   /bUwt/ _ _ _ _   /bu'n/ _ _ _ _ _ _
/klOwz/ _ _ _ _ _ _ _   /klOwThiNg/ _ _ _ _ _ _ _ _   /kOwt/ _ _ _ _
/kolEr/ _ _ _ _ _ _   /dres/ _ _ _ _ _   /gluv/ _ _ _ _ _
/hat/ _ _ _   /jakit/ _ _ _ _ _ _   /jEynz/ _ _ _ _ _
/Awtfit/ _ _ _ _ _ _   /skArf/ _ _ _ _ _   /poket/ _ _ _ _ _ _
/ShErt/ _ _ _ _ _   /ShUw/ _ _ _ _   /skErt/ _ _ _ _ _
/slEyv/ _ _ _ _ _ _   /sUwt/ _ _ _ _   /swedEr/ _ _ _ _ _ _ _
/undErwAyr/ _ _ _ _ _ _ _ _ _ _ /yUniform/ _ _ _ _ _ _ _   /wAyr/ _ _ _ _

 **How can you get four suits for a dollar?**
Buy a deck of cards.

Chapter Three   Word Search   Transcriptions

/bodEy/ Body

```
I L N R A R W B G U C P G Q J N W A J M
M R G G N E T A J Z U F T J K M E Z N M
Y O R Q I D E C Z E A S L X X D K C R T
G G U S E L E K A B M U H T N O D A K T
X A V T V U T F A I G F H G O O A O P G
D N A H H O H Y Z Z F E Y T U W S W F O
D M L C G H J P Q E C S L Y L V R E L B
S L O C Y S D T U H F M T Y N I V F K W
B H D A E D T G E R N R J S A J O M P B
T A X Y S G N S T N I A R H I O Z M S N
B C E M S O T L S V M O N P T R E B K J
R I U I T S P I N E O L J T Z H W E I T
R G H E A D Z D X Q G C L U N G C E N N
Y T S U U M U S T V O F A V K L I D Y K
U M F H K D Y H V W J O S N R C E X J U
```

/armz/ _ _ _ _   /bak/ _ _ _ _   /Chest/ _ _ _ _ _
/Iyz/ _ _ _ _   /f^t/ _ _ _ _   /gumz/ _ _ _ _
/hAyr/ _ _ _ _   /hand/ _ _ _ _   /hed/ _ _ _ _
/jo/ _ _ _   /nEy/ _ _ _ _   /leg/ _ _ _
/luNg/ _ _ _ _   /mAwTH/ _ _ _ _ _   /nek/ _ _ _
/nOwz/ _ _ _ _   /ShOwldEr/ _ _ _ _ _ _ _ _   /skin/ _ _ _ _
/spIyn/ _ _ _ _ _   /tEyTH/ _ _ _ _ _   /THum/ _ _ _ _ _
/tuNg/ _ _ _ _ _ _   /vAyn/ _ _ _ _   /rist/ _ _ _ _ _

 What do you call 100 rabbits jumping backward?
A receding hair line.

© Judy Thompson 2011   www.ThompsonLanguageCenter.com

Chapter Three   Word Search   Transcriptions

/frUwt/ Fruit

```
W T P G N A X N X S L K Q P H E I G H I
T A I A V O Z F T L Q T B X N N M R C W
J F T A P O M R E L P P A E N I P A A I
X H U E R A A E R A E P N I S R H P E K
Z G T A R W Y H L M B P A L C A F E P H
B I N L B M D A I L O X N W L T L F Y X
Y G H E J X E E Z J Y S A T H C I R E Q
E T R E X P V L I A E R O N M E M U H H
S R E P I W D U O I P Y R V B N E I S H
Y P K D W K Q R R N V P H E A Q V T T J
B L U E B E R R I E S P L D B R I U T P
P A Z D S W E F M A N G O E P P X Q P Y
D E L B T H G R A P E S U O T G S L W U
V E E H C Y L V Z Z W W P D Q A U A H O
E H K G Z F V Q F L H X O E C M D W R Y
```

/apul/ _ _ _ _ _   /bunanu/ _ _ _ _ _ _   /blUwberEyz/ _ _ _ _ _ _ _ _ _ _
/CherEyz/ _ _ _ _ _ _ _ _ /dAyt/ _ _ _ _   /fig/ _ _ _
/grAypfrUwt/ _ _ _ _ _ _ _ _ _ _ /grAyps/ _ _ _ _ _ _   /gwovu/ _ _ _ _ _
/kEywEy/ _ _ _ _   /lemun/ _ _ _ _ _   /lIym/ _ _ _ _
/lEyChEy/ _ _ _ _ _ _   /mangOw/ _ _ _ _ _   /nektErEyn/ _ _ _ _ _ _ _ _ _
/Orenj/ _ _ _ _ _ _   /pupIyu/ _ _ _ _ _ _   /pEyCh/ _ _ _ _ _
/pAyr/ _ _ _ _   /pIynapul/ _ _ _ _ _ _ _ _   /plum/ _ _ _ _
/rasberEy/ _ _ _ _ _ _ _ _ /stroberEy/ _ _ _ _ _ _ _ _ _ _ /wodErmelun/ _ _ _ _ _ _ _ _ _ _

What happens when a banana sees a ghost?
The banana splits

Chapter Three   Word Search   Transcriptions

/vej tubul/ Vegetable

```
V A N H Z L X E U O J X W Z B Q S C E Z
O Q T R Q R G L E T T U C E H P F A L S
T C N G O A C P E A S V E S R F X U A J
R U H T B C W C X T R T I O R V L L K B
S N R B N G I F W O S D U N F B A I U Z
K S A N C A Z L S P A T B G H E G F N B
J C V T I Z L D R R S R P I C A L L M S
C N B E B P E P B A O I Y E O N Z O F P
R E B M U C U C G C G N M A P S W W K I
S Q U A S H E P C G I I N C M P L E Y N
T O R R A C L O U H E H B S R A E R S A
E C S C A E L E Z D Q C N O I N O R Z C
P E X L K I C R X H B C N L S C S E S H
V Y X P P R Q U B K L U T O B I T N K U
D H L O F I B Z K L R Z O X Q J R C X K
```

/bEynz/ _ _ _ _ _   /bEyts/ _ _ _ _ _   /brokulEy/ _ _ _ _ _ _ _ _
/ro /kabuj/ _ _ _ _ _ _ _   /karuts/ _ _ _ _ _ _ _   /kolEyflAwEr/ _ _ _ _ _ _ _ _ _ _ _
/kOrn/ _ _ _ _   /kyUwkumbEr/ _ _ _ _ _ _ _ _   /egplant/ _ _ _ _ _ _ _ _
/gArlik/ _ _ _ _ _ _   /kAyl/ _ _ _ _   /kelp/ _ _ _ _
/ledus/ _ _ _ _ _ _ _   /unyun/ _ _ _ _ _   /pEyz/ _ _ _ _
/pepErz/ _ _ _ _ _ _ _   /putAydu/ _ _ _ _ _ _   /radiSh/ _ _ _ _ _ _
/spinuCh/ _ _ _ _ _ _ _   /sprAwts/ _ _ _ _ _ _ _   /skwoSh/ _ _ _ _ _ _
/tErnup/ _ _ _ _ _ _   /yam/ _ _ _   /zUwkEynEy/ _ _ _ _ _ _ _ _

 **How do you make gold soup?**
Add fourteen karats.

© Judy Thompson 2011   www.ThompsonLanguageCenter.com

/ɑnɪmul/ Animal

```
T M A Z E E R H F D C B S S V H Z E P R
O L P L L T T A V R O O M N P X S L E W
A X A T V U I U E P O N G A Q Y G E E F
D H R I M R A B G B E G K K P I D P H L
W U F K X K R L B O D S M E R N S H S O
T S T I G E R U L A D O U A Y G O A T W
S R P M E Y C U S I R W F O D D U N K X
G I P X D A Q V O F G F J V M R I T A F
C J N I T G T W O T E A R Y O A W U B V
X M Q H Z A X B D J U H T W N Z B O M D
E O M P Y C J Z H O I C M O J I K N J B
M O N K E Y P Y P N K Y U O R L N I I C
N E K C I H C W O E S R O H O V I R O V
N O I L J P L O I W L B G B H S D N L E
B D V J T J I C P C K H Q K N C E F Y H
```

/aligʌydɛr/ _ _ _ _ _ _ _ _ _   /bʌyr/ _ _ _ _   /bɛrd/ _ _ _ _
/kat/ _ _ _   /ʧɪkun/ _ _ _ _ _ _ _   /kʌw/ _ _ _
/dɛyr/ _ _ _ _   /dog/ _ _ _   /doŋkɛy/ _ _ _ _ _ _
/elufant/ _ _ _ _ _ _ _   /frog/ _ _ _ _   /jɛraf/ _ _ _ _ _ _ _
/gOwt/ _ _ _ _   /hOrs/ _ _ _ _ _   /lɪyun/ _ _ _ _
/lɪzɛrd/ _ _ _ _ _ _   /muŋkɛy/ _ _ _ _ _ _   /mUws/ _ _ _ _ _
/mʌws/ _ _ _ _ _   /pig/ _ _ _   /rabɪt/ _ _ _ _ _ _
/rɪynOw/ _ _ _ _ _   /ʃɛyp/ _ _ _ _ _   /snʌyk/ _ _ _ _ _
/tɪygɛr/ _ _ _ _ _   /tOwd/ _ _ _ _   /tɛrkɛy/ _ _ _ _ _ _
/tɛrdul/ _ _ _ _ _ _   /wʌyl/ _ _ _ _ _   /w^lf/ _ _ _ _

Chapter Three   Word Search   Transcriptions

/skUwl wErdz/ School Words

```
G E O G R A P H Y R R H Z J W S E K R P
H I S T O R Y D A E L O D S J T M O H M
T G G P O W R M T S I M K P E U H O S U
S A N E H A M H P Z C E M N R D N B S S
J W A S O A G A S C N W S U B E A K G I
B M Y B R I F O L E E O T C T N K R H C
H S S G L X A E T P P R Z I I T T O G N
Q B E H S Q S O E U H K C A W E F W N E
Y Z G M F M P D X L T A H C A C N C P P
K I G N I L L E P S B R B C B Y E C J B
H K P C F B J V D C U A H E S M A X E Z
R E S A R E O L L E E L T T B O O K S
A S P Z X H H R E W R R X L A X W I I Q
U L T P R W E R E E L C H A Y M S E K R
A S T Z D K A N S D F C F I S S J I Q K
```

/alfubet/ _____   /bOrd/ _____   /b^ks/ _____
/bOrd/ _____   /EyrAysEr/ _____   /jEyografEy/ _____
/grAydz/ _____   /gramEr/ _____   /hIylIydEr/ _____
/histrEy/ _____   /hOwmwErk/ _____ /maTH/ ____
/mUwzik/ _____   /pen/ ___   /pensul/ _____
/funedik/ _____   /rUwlEr/ _____   /sIyens/ _____
/speliNg/ _____   /stUwdent/ _____   /silabul/ _____
/tEyChEr/ _____   /egzamz/ _____   /wErkb^k/ _____

What's pronoun?
In favour of nouns.

Chapter Three   Word Search   Transcriptions

/sIyuns/ Science

```
T N W K M H Q R Y V F F S S C I S Y H P
X C O K R U J Q C Y E H O I E C A P S A
Z T S R A A V N K Z T N V R D T T K P T
G Z E N T C U O A E W I U W M N E F R A
Y B T L Y C R Q N B H R L S S U L Y I D
G U L W E G E A S T R O N A U T L H S V
M N U Q A S L L N P D N Y W B W I A M O
M H O N I P C E E X J R C N V M T J A O
Y I I T E M M O E L U C E L O M E S M C
O S Z A O I K H P C S R C T A J I U E I
M B R F R R J B R E Q F L H R S M E T L
P T C E E W P E Z G W M I H A Y R L S U
H O P E L E M E N T K X P L A A O C Y E
S X G A L A X Y J J L E H S M X L O U S Q
E V W Z H I I E J D W U E W Z S N N L H
```

/astrunot/ _____   /dAydu/ ____   /ErTH/ _____
/Eyklips/ _____   /Eylektron/ _____   /elumunt/ _____
/ekspAyrimunt/ _____   /fOrmyUwlu/ _____   /galuksEy/ _____
/mErkyErEy/ _____   /molekyUwl/ _____   /nUwklEyus/ _____
/Organism/ _____   /fiziks/ _____   /planut/ _____
/prizm/ _____   /prOwton/ _____   /kwantum/ _____
/kwArk/ _____   /sadulIyt/ _____   /spAys/ _____
/sistum/ _____   /teleskOwp/ _____   /vEynus/ _____

 **Why did Mars and Earth collide in their trip around the sun?**
They didn't planet well.

© Judy Thompson 2011   207   www.ThompsonLanguageCenter.com

Chapter Three	Word Search	Transcriptions

/envIyErmunt/ Environment

```
T Z B T Q O B E H Q R Y Y S W N T S R D
A O G T Z J L R M U T T L B E O F L C R
T W O O F C E U E V R A I G W I I D O O
I P N F Y C Y T W G C R Y V H U K H N U
B E E C O P Y A D I A X I E X A C D S G
A T E L A C Q R M F O B T C N I T X E H
H R O P L A N E T V Y T R J A Z T Q R T
V G E R L C H P V V B P M A Q N R D V B
Y E R L N C S M L A B O L G G F E F E A
N A U E G A D E R Z X H W E A T H E R F
M R T B D N D T P O L L U T I O N L U Q
Y T A K L U U O Q B A T O G X D I T B I
T H N L K M C J J Z Z G V G K P U H Q Y
Y M Z V O E Q E A D B R B Q U R A R F Y
Y S Y R I S M E S U E R H W E G L N B F
```

/kemikulz/ _ _ _ _ _ _ _ _ _   /kunsErv/ _ _ _ _ _ _ _ _   /drAwt/ _ _ _ _ _ _ _

/ErTH/ _ _ _ _ _   /EykolujEy/ _ _ _ _ _ _ _   /ekstiNgkt/ _ _ _ _ _ _ _

/fyUwChEr/ _ _ _ _ _ _   /gArbij/ _ _ _ _ _ _ _   /glOwbul/ _ _ _ _ _ _

/habutat/ _ _ _ _ _ _ _   /hErukAyn/ _ _ _ _ _ _ _ _   /juNgul/ _ _ _ _ _ _

/nAyChEr/ _ _ _ _ _ _   /oksujin/ _ _ _ _ _ _   /OwzOwn/ _ _ _ _ _

/planut/ _ _ _ _ _ _   /pulUwShun/ _ _ _ _ _ _ _ _ _   /rEysIykul/ _ _ _ _ _ _ _

/rEydUws/ _ _ _ _ _ _   /rEyUwz/ _ _ _ _ _   /sOwlEr/ _ _ _ _ _

/tempuChEr/ _ _ _ _ _ _ _ _ _ _ _   /tOrnAydOw/ _ _ _ _ _ _ _   /weThEr/ _ _ _ _ _ _ _

 **What did the ocean say to the beach?**
Nothing, it just waved.

© Judy Thompson 2011	208	www.ThompsonLanguageCenter.com

Chapter Three   Word Search   Transcriptions

/medikul/ Medical

```
C H P B F C H L O S Z B G Y N H U M A D
J O Z R S P A T R O X O L R A G N N B I
K X N G A C H R N C U R E E I U X G D G
K E E S I C Y G R E L L A G C O B V O E
R W H S C E T N N E M C U R I C A H M S
O O Y T S I A I G E O T P U T G U Q E T
S H T R A I O A C P E A N S P E J R N I
P D U C L E S U E E G D S I O L Z E E O
P N A M O S R R S O S N L L O K Y M I N
U D E U A D A B Z O E Z W E L L N E S S
B N U M C T A R T E R Y L S G Z J D J H
T A Z R I D L C Z N O I S I V O Z Y M M
A B F O Q U C E J T S R W X Z H A J U J
Q P N I K S X V U Z W Z P F Q O M C T I
E E L A T I P S O H Z E B H Q O Y U Z B
```

/abdumun/ _____   /Aylmunt/ _____ __   /alErjEy/ _____
/ArdErEy/ _____   / brEyTh/ _____   /konShus/ _____
/kof/ _____   /kyUwr/ ____   /dIyjesjun/ _____
/dokdEr/ _____   /hospidul/ _____   /masoZh/ _____
/nEydul/ _____   /nErs/ _____   /Oynmunt/ _____
/opErAyShun/ _____   /optiShun/ _____   /fizikul/ _____
/prakdis/ _____   /remudEy/ _____   /snEyz/ _____
/sEerjurEy/ _____   /viZhun/ _____   /welnes/ _____

 **How long should a doctor practice medicine?**
Until he gets it right.

Chapter Three   Word Search   Transcriptions

/wErkplAys/ Workplace

```
P E T W M P V F R A C N T Y J S W S I N
L M R E A A N I U E G O P E E C Z U N C
U U M I N C N T Q I T O M R K C D L T E
M S C V U R O A E M C N V P H R K Y E K
B E P R F M I R G O T I E G U M A U R J
E R W E A O O Z T E C V P P G T P M E Y
R X T T C F V O D E R Z T H R K E M S M
J H I N T Y H B E N E F I T S A P R T O
A O L I U P N T T R O P X E S L C Y G N
N O C S R B Q A P S M M S V O Q R U W O
L V H F E V L F P I H E O Y R A T S B C
T N U O C C A H U M D I E E L R S R F E
H Y Q I V U E A I B O E F A R E T I R E
N A I C I N H C E T K C S T H X K K O S
K C L C I R E U T X W U Z F O R E M A N
```

/u**kAw**nt/ _____   /odu**mAy**Shun/ _____   /**be**nefits/ _____
/**kAr**puntEr/ _____   /**kum**punEy/ _____   /**kum**pyUwdEr/ _____
/Ey**ko**numEy/ _____   /em**plO**yEy/ _____   /**eks**pOrt/ _____
/**fO**run/ _____   /**fO**rmun/ _____   /**in**trust/ _____
/**in**tErvUw/ _____   /**man**ujEr/ _____   /manyUw**fak**ChEr/ _____
/**mAr**kut/ _____   /**fOw**dukopEy/ _____   /**plu**mEr/ _____
/**re**zumAy/ _____   /**ru**tIyEr/ _____   /**sa**lurEy/ _____
/**sEr**vis/ _____   /**Shift**/ _____   /tek**ni**Shun/ _____

What do you get when you cross a plumber with a ballerina?
A tap dancer

Line Match

Grammar Words

Match the words in the first column to one that rhymes in the second. (Solution is on page 233.)

Verb: to be

I'm	freeze
you're	stair
he's	floor
she's	clear
we're	time
they're	sir
were	please

Future

I'll	nail
he'll	cool
she'll	style
we'll	steel
you'll	meal
they'll	wheel

 How do you scramble eggs?
g-e-s-g

Ordinary Words

Match the words in the first column to one that rhymes in the second. The first is done for you. (Solution is on page 233.)

does	/**duz**/	right	/**rIyt**/
said	/**sed**/	buzz	/**buz**/
half	/**haf**/	rock	/**rok**/
busy	/**biz**Ey/	great	/**grAyt**/
quite	/**kwIyt**/	or	/**Or**/
talk	/**tok**/	wild	/**wIyld**/
Mrs.	/**mi**siz/	love	/**luv**/
of	/**uv**/	try it	/**trIyut**/
suit	/**sUwt**/	boot	/**bUwt**/
eight	/**Ayt**/	laugh	/**laf**/
through	/**THrUw**/	misses	/**mi**siz/
Mr.	/**mis**dEr/	go	/**gOw**/
was	/**wuz**/	sister	/**sis**dEr/
child	/**ChIyld**/	fuzz	/**fuz**/
drawer	/**drOr**/	stuff	/**stuf**/
enough	/Ey**nuf**/	you	/**yUw**/
lose	/**lUwz**/	Is he?	/**iz**Ey/
young	/**yuNg**/	red	/**red**/
quiet	/**kwIyut**/	sung	/**suNg**/
sew	/**sOw**/	news	/**nUwz**/

What is round and bad tempered?
A vicious circle

Practice Native Speaking

The Little Cares
by Elizabeth Barrett Browning

The little cares that fretted me,	/Thu lidel kAyrz That fredid mEy
I lost them yesterday	Iy lost Them yesdErdAy
Among the fields above the sea,	amuNg Thu fEyldz abuv The sEy
Among the winds at play;	amuNg Thu windz at plAy
Among the lowing of the herds,	amuNg The lOwiNg uv Thu hErdz
The rustling of the trees,	Thu rusliNg uv The trEyz
Among the singing of the birds,	amuNg The siNgiNg uv The bErdz
The humming of the bees.	Thu humiNg uv The bEyz/
The foolish fears of what may happen	/Thu fUwlish fEyrz uv wut mAy hapen
I cast them all away	Iy cast Them ol awAy
Among the clover-scented grass,	amuNg The clOwvEr sentid gras
Among the new-mown hay;	amuNg Thu nUw-mOwn hAy
Among the husking of the corn	amuNg Thu huskiNg uv Thu kOrn
Where drowsy poppies nod,	wAyr drAwzEy popEyz nod
Where ill thoughts die and good are born,	wAyr il THots dIy and g^d Ar bOrn
Out in the fields with God.	Awt in Thu fEyldz wiTH god/

Indian Summer
By William Wilfred Campbell

Along the line of smoky hills	/uloNg Thu lIyn uv smOwkEy hilz
The crimson forest stands,	Thu krimzun fOrest standz
And all the day the blue-jay calls	and ol dAy loNg Thu blUw-jAy kolz
Throughout the autumn lands.	THrUwAwt Thu odum landz/
Now by the brook the maple leans,	/nAw bIy Thu br^k Thu mAypul lEynz
With all his glory spread;	wiTH ol hiz glOrEy spred
And all the sumacs on the hills	and ol Thu sUwmaks on Thu hilz
Have turned their green to red.	hav tErnd ThAyr grEyn tUw red/
Now, by great marshes wrapt in mist,	/nAw bIy grAt mArShiz rapt in mist
Or past some river's mouth,	Or past sum riverz mAwTH
Throughout the long still autumn day	ThrUwAwt Thu loNg stil otum dAy
Wild birds are flying south.	wIyld bErdz Ar flIyiNg sAwTH/

English is Stupid Page 65

Cry Wolf

Once upon a time, a lonely shepherd boy sat watching his sheep. Nothing unusual ever happened on the quiet hillside, so the boy decided to play a trick on the townspeople. He cried, *Wolf! Wolf! Wolf!* The villagers ran up the hill armed with sticks to drive the wolf away. There was no wolf.

Everyone was angry that the boy was just pulling their leg, but the boy enjoyed his little joke. The next day he cried, *Wolf! Wolf! The wolf is eating the sheep!* Again the villagers ran to help. The boy laughed at them.

On the third day, a big hungry wolf attacked the sheep. The terrified boy screamed for help, but no one came. The wolf ate all the sheep. The boy realized too late the importance of telling the truth.

/krIy w^lf/

/wuns upon u tIym, u lOwnlEy ShepErd bOy, sat woChiNg hiz ShEyp. noTHiNg unyUwZhuwul evEr hapend on Thu kwIyet hilsIyd, sOw The bOy dusIydid tUw plAy u trik on Thu tAwnzpEypul. hEy krIyd, w^lf w^lf w^lf. Thu vilijErz ran up Thu hil Armd wiTH stiks tUw drIyv Thu w^lf uwAy. ThAyr wuz nOw w^lf.

evrEywun wuz aNgrEy That Thu bOy wuz just p^liNg ThAyr leg, but Thu bOy enjOyd hiz lidel jOwk. Thu nekst dAy hEy krIyd, w^lf w^lf. Thu w^lf iz EydiNg Thu ShEyp. ugen Thu vilijErz ran tUw help. Thu bOy laft at Them.

on Thu THErd dAy u big huNgrEy w^lf utakt Thu ShEyp. Thu terifIyd bOy skrEymd fOr help but nOw wun kAym. Thu w^lf Ayt ol Thu ShEyp. Thu bOy rEyulIyzd tUw lAyt Thu impOrns uv teliNg Thu trUwTH/

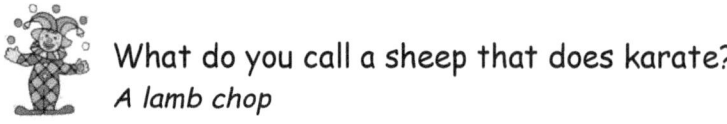

What do you call a sheep that does karate?
A lamb chop

APPENDIX 1

Language Index

Arabic

Consonant sounds: 41, 45, 46, 47, 44, 50, 55, 59, 76, 83, 85, 94, 95

Vowel sounds: 121, 122, 124, 125, 127, 134/135, 138/139, 142/143, 146/147, 154/155, 168, 169, 171, 173

Chinese

Consonant sounds: 41, 45, 46, 47, 48, 50, 55, 59, 72, 76, 82, 83, 91, 94, 95

Vowel sounds: 121, 122, 124, 128, 142/143, 146/147, 148/149, 163, 168, 169, 171, 173

French

Consonant sounds: 41, 45, 46, 47, 50, 51, 55, 59, 70, 83, 85, 88, 95

Vowel sounds: 124, 127, 142/143, 146/147, 150/151, 158/159, 168, 169, 171, 173

Hindi

Consonant sounds: 41, 45, 46, 47, 49, 50, 52, 55, 59, 77, 78, 83, 88, 95

Vowel sounds: 122, 124, 127, 142/143, 146/147, 150/151, 158/159, 168, 169, 171, 173

Japanese

Consonant sounds: 41, 45, 46, 47, 48, 49, 50, 59, 72, 76, 83, 85, 88, 91, 94, 95

Vowel sounds: 121, 122, 124, 142/143, 146/147, 150/151, 158/159, 167, 168, 169, 171, 173

Korean

Consonant sounds: 41, 45, 46, 47, 48, 50, 55, 59, 72, 76, 83, 88, 91, 94, 95

Vowel sounds: 121, 122, 124, 128, 142/143, 146/147, 148/149, 163, 168, 169, 171, 173

Spanish

Consonant sounds: 41, 45, 46, 47, 50, 51, 52, 55, 59, 64, 65, 70, 71, 79, 83, 84, 88, 95

Vowel Sounds: 122, 123, 124, 125, 127, 138/139, 142/143, 146/147, 150/151, 158/159, 166, 168, 169, 171, 173

APPENDIX 2

English is Stupid, copy of page 34

Consonant Sounds

There are **24** consonant sounds in English. Consonants are **stopped** or restricted sounds. [Stage directions – chop your right hand onto the palm of your left in an emphatic motion with each sound – /b/, /d/, /f/ – finished or stopped sounds.] Students will get the idea.

The consonant sounds in the **English Phonetic Alphabet** are featured on page 35. *Capitals* indicate sounds represented by pairs of symbols.

FYI

This is not a pronunciation textbook. That said, there are some useful insights into pronunciation included as basic information. Fuller explanations and exercises are available in an array of pronunciation texts like *Pronunciation Pals* and *Sounds Great*.

Sister Sounds

Pairs of sounds that are place in the mouth are **sister** One **sister** is made by mouth in a given position, drawing air *in* from the same sound from the throat.

formed in exactly the same **sounds**. It is useful to know. blowing air out from the and its **sister** is made by mouth position, creating a

Air Out   **Air In**

/p/	pig	/b/	big
/t/	to	/d/	do
/k/	came	/g/	game
/f/	fan	/v/	van
/s/	said	/z/	zed
/TH/	thigh	/Th/	thy
/Ch/	cheap	/j/	jeep
/Sh/	shone	/zh/	genre

APPENDIX 3

Solutions for Chapter One

Consonant Hunt – Food
(page 55)

ham /h/, ribs /r /, vegetable /v/, pasta /p/, cake /k/, bread /d/, melon /l/, yogurt /y/, meat /m/, beef au jus /Zh/, tuna /t /, string beans /Ng/

fish /f/, corn on the cob /Th/, mushroom /Sh/, tangerine /j/, zucchini /z/, celery /s/, chicken /Ch/, nuts /n/, broth /TH/, cabbage /b/, eggplant /g/, wheat /w/

Consonant Hunt – Clothing
(page 56)

dress /d/, suit /s/, cap /k/, windbreaker /r/, scarf /f/, undies /z/, handbag /h/, beige slacks /Zh/, uniform /n/, leggings /Ng/, shirt /Sh/, yellow pj's /y/

gloves /g/, leather jacket /Th /, pants /p/, sweater /w/, tuxedo /t/, trench coat /Ch/, vest /v/, umbrella /l/, thermal socks /TH /, jeans /j/, briefcase /b/, mittens /m/

Consonant Hunt – Body
(page 57)

head /h/, back /b/, chest /Ch/, elbow /w/, stomach /k/, nose /z/, teeth /t/, leg /l/, finger /Ng/, mouth /m/, foot /f/, shoulder /Sh/

spine /p/, eye /y/, vein /v/, jaw /j/, skin /s/, neck /n/, thumb /TH /, breathe /Th/, hand /d, arm/r/, gums /g/, vision /Zh/

Consonant Discrimination
(page 58)

girl / g`/, giant /j/, cough /f/, cello /Ch/, sugar /Sh/, usual /Zh/, nation /Sh/, nature /Ch/, education /j/, question /j/, answer Ø, who /h/, when /w/, birthday /TH/, sign Ø, busy /z/, vehicle Ø, names /z/, Asia /Zh/, comb /m/

sing /Ng/, ocean /Sh/, half Ø, antique /k/, Christmas Ø, passion /Sh/, toilet /t/, buffet /Ay/, orange /j/, whale /w/, arctic Ø, please /z/, ache /k/, choir /kw/, dogs /z/, cats /s/, walk Ø, exit /ks/ or /gz/, February Ø, century /s/

campaign Ø, quarter /kw/, six /ks/, north /TH/, league /g/, pleasure / Zh/, racquet /k/, pizza /t/, union /y/, honor Ø, wished /t/, danced /s/, laughed /f/, asked /t/, social /Sh/, button Ø, Europe /y/, garage /Zh/, both /TH/, print /n/

Terrible T – Advanced
(page 59)

time /t/; water /d/; quality /d/; spaghetti /d/; photo /d/; photography /t/; nature /Ch/; internet Ø; city /d/; exciting /d/; listen Ø; little /d/; written Ø; soften Ø; tsunami Ø; thyme /t/; pizza /t/; temperature /t/, /Ch/; Christian /j/; tomato /t/, /d/; photograph /d/; Dakota /d/; mitten Ø; mountain Ø; united /d/

position /Sh/; start /t/, /ₜ/; started /t/, /d/; potato /t/, /d/; international Ø, /Sh/; furniture /Ch/; bracelet /ₜ/; computer /d/; attractive /t/ /d/; what /ₜ/; debt /ₜ/; retire /t/; Tuesday /t/; whistle Ø; Thompson /t/; Connecticut /d/, /ₜ/; counter Ø; intelligent /t/, /ₜ/; contrast /t/, /ₜ/; fountain Ø; British /d/; content /t/, /ₜ/; capital /d/; asthma Ø; sentence Ø

Singular/Plural
(page 62)

/s/ skirts, coats, caps, shirts, backpacks, undershirts, raincoats, belts, hats, vests, bracelets, boots

/z/ scarves, gloves, stockings, jeans, sneakers, ties, umbrellas, shoes, hair bands, earrings, sweaters

/iz/ blouses, glasses, briefcases, purses, necklaces, dresses

Simple Past Tense of Regular Verbs – Basic
(page 64)

/t/ looked, asked, wished, cooked, talked, brushed, danced, baked

/d/ moved, spelled, turned, cried, studied, shaved, lived, played

/id/ reported, handed, added, tasted, planted, started, waited, stated

Simple Past Tense Regular Verbs – Advanced
(page 65)

/t/ relaxed, erased, finished, attached, typed, videotaped, laughed

/d/ unscrambled, manufactured, exchanged, vacuumed, fertilized, capitalized, brainstormed, supervised

/id/ operated, texted, comprehended, inserted, computed, littered, befriended, requested, immigrated

Mystery Match Series
(page 66)

/b/ Basic	/h/ Basic	/m/ Basic	/r/ Basic
beard	happy	minutes	wrist
brother	who	mop	ranch
babies	hand	milk	rings
bricks	he	mall	rhino
bathroom	heavy	melon	radish
buy	house	mustard	wrong
because	help	medicine	rhymes
bank	hair	Monday	raccoon
boats	health	mitten	raspberries
bones	humor	May	rope
blond	hotdog	margarine	rake
bed	highways	morning	wreath
bicycle	history	mechanic	rye
beet	hunger	mouth	reverse

/d/ Basic	/j/ Advanced	/n/ Basic	/v/ Basic
door	June	nephew	verb
dress	jujubes	noon	vegetable
Dad	gym	knife	vegetables
doughnut	giant	noun	veterinarian
duck	education	knuckles	vote
drain	jam	needle	vertical
dentist	fudge	neck	vines
dollar	question	numbers	visa
dirty	soldiers	news	verse
desks	general	November	Venus
dog	joke	nurse	van
draw	jargon	nose	voice
drank	George	pneumonia	visitor
dye	engine	knee	volunteer
			vocabulary

/g/ Basic	/kw/ Basic	/p/ Basic	/w/ Basic
glove	queen	play	went
grape	choir	please	windows
good	quiet	part	one
green	quarter	pronounce	waist
garden	quartz	plate	white
ghosts	quarrel	potato	Wednesday
game	quilt	puppy	where
grammar	quiz	presents	worker
giggle	Quebec	pen	waterfall
golf	quit	practice	wise
gas	quick	paid	wheels
good-bye	quality	puzzle	once
get	quake	pineapple	wax
groceries		purple	walk

/y/ Basic	recognize	shower	pink
yellow	easy	shine	single
yogurt	exercise	shapes	English
Europe	clothes	shaving	sink
year		she	strong
university	/Ch/ Advanced	shop	hung
yearn	chair	champagne	orangutan
U	watch	shampoo	language
yesterday	chapter		drink
yam	chimney	/TH/ Basic	long
uniform	cappuccino	Thursday	singing
ewe	nature	thirsty	skunk
yoga	charcoal	thank you	
yes	change	think	/Zh/ Advanced
unicorn	picture	thermometer	garage
	hatch	thigh	beige
/z/	cello	threw	television
Advanced	cheese	third	usual
scissors	fracture	thief	Taj Mahal
zebra	sculpture	thread	azure
hers		thin	pleasure
size	/Sh/ Basic	thistle	rouge
zipper	shy	thirty-three	massage
exams	should	thumb	mirage
roses	sugar		genre
seize	sheep	/Ng/ Advanced	Echinacea
plagiarize	sure	triangle	corsage
example	chef	king	Asia

Consonant Sound Mazes
(page 86)

/b/ butter, barn, table, October, about, brown, problem, believe, public, boring, bladder, harbor, better, blink, cable, balloon, rebel, button, barber, bologna, abdomen, cucumber, embrace

/d/ water, pretty, potato, arctic, reported, forty, little, photograph, automatic, hospital, system, poetic, turtle, yesterday, lettuce, thirsty, computer, butter, Saturday, fifty, political, daughter, justice, society, spaghetti

/f/ phone, pharmacy, laugh, enough, trophy, physics, nephew, trough, graph, physician, symphony, cough, phonetic, photo, laughter, rough, paragraph, phase, tough, physio, phat

/k/ kettle, cloth, quick, stomach, box, school, basket, cocoa, exchange, square, broccoli, coffee, barbecue, chocolate, tickle, fax, column, explain, quiche, chemical, cucumber, access, monkey

/l/ - lemon, lake, call, purple, flower, lung, ladder, temple, left, whale, fill, lottery, list, until, clap, plate, willow, letter, goal, yellow, length, hotel, linen, kettle, outlet, polish, light, world, welcome

/m/ money, mother, March, men, mouth, mittens, market, month, mustard, merry, milk, mobile, music, mist, memory, mango, million, muffin, meat, match, moon

/n/ nine, never, knee, net, nice, knock, noun, nurse, know, note, neck, need, knot, nephew, nerve, needle, knuckle, north, knife, night, nothing

/r/ ribbon, carrot, birth, angry, carpet, turn, author, radish, camera, rabbit, wreath, protest, church, drought, quartz, worth, unicorn, trouble, address, wrist, regular, serve, smart, bird, river, rooster, short

/Th/ the, then, mother, that, weather, these, other, together, this, bother, than, either, though, father, they, northern, neither, those, brother, thy, they're

The *Silent Consonants* Riddle – Answers
(page 96)

write w, half l, knife k, answer w, walk l, listen t, thumb b, receipt p, hour h, ache h, Wednesday d, two w, know k, school h, plumber b, what h, right gh, debt b, island s, February r, clothes th, scissors c, though gh, when h, sign g, science – first c, government – first n, autumn n, psychology p, h, asthma th

The *H* Riddle
(page 97) — All the underlined h's are silent.

Invisible Consonants
(page 98)

yunicorn, powet, liyon, wone, quiyet, thingk, fuwel, yEurope, iyEron, cyucumber, yuniform, kowala, highyer, beyautiful, pangcake, fluwid, fyew, wonce, yunit, piyano, cyute, powem, tiyre, somepthing, Cyuba, ideya

Cry Wolf Sound Search Consonants
(page 109)

These are some of the possible answers – there are many more

/b/	boy, big, but	/s/	once, sat next
/d/	decided, drive, day	/t/	time, laughed, terrified
/f/	wolf, laughed, terrified	/v/	ever, villagers, drive
/g/	leg, again, big	/w/	once, watching, wolf
/h/	his, happened, hungry	/y/	boy, play, enjoyed
/j/	villagers, joke, just	/z/	townspeople, realized
/k/	quiet, trick, screamed	/Sh/	shepherd, sheep
/l/	lonely, hillside, pulling	/Ch/	watching
/m/	time, armed, came	/TH/	nothing, third, truth,
/n/	once, nothing, ran	/Th/	the, there, them
/p/	upon, shepherd, play	/Ng/	nothing, angry, hungry
/r/	ever, there, trick	/Zh/	unusual

Solutions for Chapter Two

VOWELS

ESL Telephone Alphabet Colors
(page 120)

ace – gray, boy – turquoise, cat – black, dog – olive, east – green, five – white, goat – yellow, house – brown, ice cream – white/green, July - white, king – pink, lemon – red, money – mustard, number – mustard, open – gold, people – green, queen – green, red – red, summer – mustard, time – white, uniform – blue, visa – green, woman – wood, x-ray – red/gray, yellow – red, zebra – green

Er – Ar – Or Pronunciation
(page 121)

shirt /Er/	park /Ar/	door /Or/	warm /Or/	store /Or/	sugar /Ar/
alarm /Ar/	court /Or/	normal /Or/	herd /Er/	organ /Or/	heart /Ar/
earth /Er/	turn /Er/	storm /Or/	certain /Er/	curtain /Er/	worth /Er/

Rhyming Words for Every Color
(page 122)

	Sound	Example						
1	/Ay/	fate	date	mate	ate	plate	hate	late
2	/a/	fat	bat	cat	sat	hat	flat	pat
3	/Ey/	feet	beat	neat	seat	sheet	eat	meet
4	/e/	fed	red	said	led	bed	dead	wed
5	/Iy/	flight	white	night	kite	might	sight	right
6	/i/	fit	knit	sit	bit	kit	pit	lit
7	/Ow/	fold	old	told	cold	sold	mould	fold
8	/o/	fought	taught	caught	got	shot	lot	pot
9	/uw/	food	mood	sued	glued	rude	crude	chewed
10	/u/	fun	run	gun	nun	bun	sun	done
11	/^/	full	pull	bull	wool			
12	/Oy/	foil	boil	soil	toil	oil	coil	broil
13	/Aw/	found	sound	pound	bound	loud	cow	how
14	/Er/	first	worst	burst	cursed	nursed	thirst	versed
15	/Ar/	far	bar	car	jar	tar	par	char
16	Or	four	more	store	for	shore	chore	door

Circle the Words that Rhyme
Basic
(page 128)

- (eight / ate) / date
- (C / he / three)
- to / no / go
- now / not / cow
- street / (heat / feet)
- (kiss / miss / hiss)

- (rose / hose / toes)
- sign / (mine / whine)
- (four / door / more)
- (you / blue / knew)
- good / hood / food
- bought / right / caught

- nut / cut / put
- park / perk / mark
- (guest / test / best)
- oil / boil / royal
- bread / bead / bed
- (bird / word / third)

Advanced
(page 129)

- (ache / break / make)
- eye / why / ski
- heard / beard / feared
- (could / wood / should)
- pair / bear / beer
- (back / plaque / yak)

- (hairy / very / marry)
- (said / fed / head)
- (come / from / gum)
- with / myth / south
- suit / suite / sweet
- (boat / wrote / vote)

- (worst / first / versed)
- (knot / lot / thought)
- her / were / there
- (oil / royal / foil)
- (fuel / school / who'll)
- mouth / south / youth

Homonym Horrors
(page 130)

1. grate
2. wait, knot
3. wood
4. pale
5. lesson, week
6. break, heal
7. hoarse
8. towed
9. Your
10. bear
11. sew, clothes
12. manners, so
13. know, I
14. pain
15. one, time
16. ants, two, by, two
17. fair
18. idle
19. hare
20. aisle

Mystery Word Match Series
(page 131)
Vowels

Gray
/Ay/ Basic
name
waitress
paper
ache
steak
face
date
rainbow
bracelet
café
train
break
weigh
today

Gray
/Ay/ Advanced
grain
operation
straight
angel
gauge
Asia
behavior
snake
population
vein
create
square
neighbor
brain

Black
/a/ Basic
apple
laugh
grass
calf
hat
can'

last
grammar
family
answer
dance
bananas
hand
language

Black
/a/ Advanced
factory
Africa
graph
elastic
alphabet
plaid
vocabulary
sandwich
scratch
understand
janitor
contraction
relax
fractions

Green
/Ey/ Basic
tea
zucchini
sleep
police
teeth
peace
sneeze
zebra
key
jeans
receipt
female
easy
piece

Green
/Ey/ Advanced
genius
machine
grease
people
triage
engineer
ski
breathe
email
degree
jalapeno
caffeine
believe
league

Red
/e/ Basic
February
cherry
bread
yellow
parent
friend
end
said
letters
penny
feather
gentle
bell
guest

Red
/e/ Advanced
regular
healthy
guess
marriage
welcome
December

treasure
electric
excellent
many
attention
leather
expert
eleven

White
/Iy/ Basic
wife
I
cry
height
child
kind
five
eye
right
pie
my
Hi
bye
thigh

White
/Iy/ Advanced
island
papaya
icicle
site
rhyme
aisle
recycle
diamond
quiet
vinyl
choir
guide
surprise
thyme

Solutions for Chapter Two, Vowels

Pink
/i/ Basic
winter
children
little
busy
kiss
sister
women
city
mystery
gift
listen
business
fingers
adding

Pink
/i/ Advanced
sibling
build
wink
hymns
income
spring
list
pretty
whistle
blisters
myth
cylinder
opinion
competition

Gold
/Ow/ basic
toast
sew
toe
gold
pony
throw
whole
open
throat
dough
tow
coat
home
nose

Gold
/Ow/ Advanced
bow
photo
shoulder
bologna
coast
spoken
beau
pneumonia
approach
zone
October
vogue
although
throne

Olive
/o/ Basic
coffee
daughter
talk
laundry
strawberry
August
water
law
song
father
broccoli
box
doctor
pocket

Olive
/o/ Advanced
economy
cauliflower
comedy
deposit
apostrophe
caught
thaws
thermometer
photographer
optometrist
conscious
thought
opera
college

Blue
/Uw/ Basic
boots
Tuesday
fruit
news
computer
school
group
uniform
you
zoo
cute
who
suit
beautiful

Blue
/Uw/ Advanced
view
fuel
bruise
juice
sewer
youth
few
route
cube
lieutenant
dew
kangaroo
through
approve

Mustard
/u/ Basic
bus
money
pumpkin
one
honey
lung
cousin
lunch
blood
country
tongue
sun
was
love

Mustard
/u/ Advanced
oven
government
funny
the
enough
stomach
once
bulb
mother
of
because
tough
come
young

Wood
/^/ Basic
push
took
woman
cook
good
football
pull
look
should
books
foot
sugar
hook
hood

Wood
/^/ Advanced
wool
soot
bush
crooked
cushions
woof
full
could
pudding
shook
wolf
cookies
stood
put

Turquoise
/Oy/ Basic
boy
coin
royal
noise
oyster
point
lawyer
joy
boil
toilet
oil
loin
toys
join

Turquoise
/Oy/ Advanced
soil
employ
moist
foil
ointment
enjoy
loyal
poison
destroy
embroidery
rejoice
boisterous

annoy
joint

Brown
/Aw/ Basic
cow
mouth
vowels
town
down
hour
sound
flowers
mouse
how
noun
house
mountain
south

Brown
/Aw/ Advanced
cloud
owl
blouse
doubt
counter
announce
ounce
fountain
boundary
clown
account
frown
pronounce
thousand

Purple
/Er/ Basic
girl
nurse
circle
verb
purse
Earth
person
worst
shirt

turkey
her
birthday
word
heard

Purple
/Er/ Advanced
insurance
Europe
curtain
thirty
surf
detergent
herd
world
were
journey
anniversary
nervous
reverse
courage

Charcoal
/Ar/ Basic
hard
heart
yard
scarf
March
guards
arms
large
farmer
garbage
cards
r
market
start

Charcoal
/Ar/ Advanced
sharpener
charge
argument
sergeant
carpet
ward

bargain
margin
Charming
martial arts
partners
guitar
departures
carton

Orange
/Or/ Basic
morning
shorts
floor
corn
organs
warm
board
storm
horse
important
warn
fourth
story
fork

Orange
/Or/ Advanced
resort
orchard
divorce
quarry
hoarse
florist
warts
fortunate
orchestra
export
cork
tornado
drawer
roar

Chapter Three Solutions Transcriptions

Vowel Sounds Mazes
(page 165)

/Ay/ **Gray** gray, day, weigh, say, hey, stay, train, ate, weight, there, away, rain, name, date, great, eight, hay, same, gate, tray, très, race

/e/ **Red** red, head, said, get, next, many, vest, guess, very, friend, bread, any, smell, nephew, N, health, exit, stretch, penny, L, west, guest, parent

/Iy/ **White** white, fight, bite, sight, side, prize, my, cycle, hide, why, find, ride, quiet, knife, right, eye, fly, height, wife, style, pie

/i/ **Pink** pink, lip, until, chin, gift, wrist, sing, trick, busy, thick, insect, women, print, build, fix, hymn, him, spring, mystery, kiss, twist

/o/ **Olive** olive, hot, coffee, on, dog, father, office, doctor, crawl, shop, shock, all, college, off, want, hall, got, bought, cot, caught, knot, naughty, collie, hospital

/Uw/ **Blue** blue, shoe, cool, new, who, you, juice, tooth, knew, suit, glue, youth, beautiful, two, dew, to, moo, flute, jewel, boot, due, soup, music, tool, queue

/u/ **Mustard** mustard, mother, from, public, tongue, must, the, hundred, country, funny, rough, does, done, come, cousin, stomach, money, was

/Aw/ **Brown** brown, cow, out, gown, south, vowel, house, howl, couch, frown, mouth, towel, ouch, allow, plough, tower, shout, powder, hour, amount, fowl, ounce, mouse,

/Er/ **Purple** purple, herd, girl, nurse, birth, work, alert, world, jerk, bird, earth, first, were, curtain, church, certain, earn, her, shirt, turtle, fur, serve, third, skirt, burst

Cry Wolf Sound Search Vowels
(page 185)

These are some of the possible answers – there are many more

/Ay/	play, their, day		/Uw/	unusual, truth, too
/a/	sat, happened, laughed		/u/	once, upon, nothing,
/Ey/	sheep, he, eating		/^/	wolf, pulling
/e/	shepherd, ever, leg		/Oy/	boy, enjoyed
/Iy/	time, quiet, cried		/Aw/	townspeople
/i/	his, trick, hill		/Er/	shepherd, third
/Ow/	lonely, joke		/Ar/	armed
/o/	watching, on		/Or/	importance

Solutions to Chapter Three

Transcriptions

Line Match – Basic
(page 188)

nine, purple, green, head, nose, cheek, nail, knuckle, palm, turkey, meat, fruit, cheese, apple, circle, square, talk, tooth, knee, lion

Line Match – Advanced
(page 189)

daughter, single, curtain, fridge, office, work, choice, patient, ghost, earth, sugar, diet, nausea, recycle, garage, woods, their, sixteen, noise, rhyme

Food – Basic
(page 190)

carrot, bread, celery, potato, cucumber, string bean, onion, garlic, coffee, cheese, butter, chicken thighs
juice, sausage, zucchini, sugar, wheat, cherries, peaches, oranges, raisins, dates, lettuce, beef au jus

Clothes – Basic
(page 191)

shirt, sweater, jeans, suit, tie, gloves, watch, blouse, raincoat, long johns, gotchies, socks
wallet, gown, uniform, dress, shorts, purse, scarf, jacket, earrings, boots, glasses, bracelet

Body – Basic
(page 192)

head, eye nose teeth, foot, mouth, knees, finger, palm, knuckle, nails, muscle
hair, throat, tongue, tummy, wrist, lungs, heart, stomach, eyebrow, freckle, forearm, ears

Numbers and Common Words
(page 193)

one, two, three, five, six, eight, twenty, thirty, forty, seventy, hundred, thousand
is, was, does, the, walk, laugh, from, we, they, of, cough, little

School Words
(page 194)

class, teacher, student, parent, paper, work, English, office, computer, quiet, screen, chair
listen, question, answer, read, write/right, alphabet, A, B, C, H, Q, success

Environment – Advanced
(page 195)

trees, birds, nature, solar, energy, pollution, garbage, recycle, compost, hydro, poison, insulate
protection, erosion, reuse, efficiency, conserve, alternative, thermal, biofuel, nuclear, power, biosphere, species

Medical – Advanced
(page 196)

allergy, therapy, vision, conscious, stitches, diabetic, benign, stethoscope, syringe, procedure, hospital, cholesterol

surgeon, dietician, paramedic, medicine, patient, hygienist, cavity, appointment, healthy, operation, clinic, physical

Workplace – Advanced
(page 197)

contract, wages, payroll, deduction, promotion, client, engineer, designer, service, electronic, mechanic, factory

security, office, operator, recruiter, interview, network, resume, options, probation, volunteer, labourer, water-cooler

Déjà Vu Transcriptions – Advanced
(page 198)

girl, giant, cough, cello, sugar, usual, nation, nature, education, question, answer, who, when, birthday, sign, busy, vehicle, names, Asia, sing, ocean, half, antique, Christmas, passion, toilet, buffet, orange, what

arctic, please, ache, choir, dogs, cats, walk, exit, February, century, campaign, quarter, six, north, league, pleasure, racquet, pizza, union, honor, wished, danced, laughed, asked, social, button, Europe, garage, both

Word Searches
Easy Beginner
(page 199)

```
P E O P L E S W A R M H + P +
+ + C + C + + C + + + O + I +
+ A + H + + P + H + + R E N +
R E A + E + + A + O + S S K +
+ I N U + + + + R + O E U + +
R + L O Y P P A H K + L O + +
+ B + + H + + + + + + + H + +
+ + + + + P + + + + + + + + +
```

blue, car, chair, happy, horse, house, park, people, phone, pink, school, warm

Food
(page 200)

```
C + + + F + P V E G E T A B L E + + C R
O + + + + E + A K C U D + W T + + A E I
O + + + + + E + S + + + H U + B B G + B
K S A L A M I B N T + E N T M B R + + S
I S N E K C I H C O A A R A A U C O R N
N E Z + + + P + + T M U L G B + + + + +
G I + U + + M + + + G L E M + + + + + +
+ R + + C + I + + O + + A + M + + + + +
+ E + + + C R + Y + + H + S A + + + + +
+ C + + + + H + + + + + + N + + + + + +
+ O + + + + S I + + + + + G + + + + + +
+ R H + + + S + N + + + + O M + + + + +
+ G S + + + + T + I + + + + E + + + + +
+ + I + + + + + U + + H G I H T + A + +
+ + F + + + + + + N + + + + + + + + T +
```

beef, cabbage, chicken, cooking, corn, duck, fish, groceries, hamburger, lamb, mango, meat, nuts, pasta, ribs, salami, salmon, shrimp, thigh, tuna, vegetable, wheat, yogurt, zucchini

Clothes
(page 201)

```
J C G S H I R T F + + + + + G N T + +
E O N T R I K S + R + + + L + O + + +
A L I + + + + + D A + + O + O T + + +
N L H + + + + + + R C V + B T + + + +
S A T U N I F O R M T E S + + + U + +
+ R O + + + U + + E T + T S H O E B + + +
R + L + + T + + K + L S + S C + + + + +
+ A C + F + + C + + E + U + O + + + + +
+ + E I + + O + + H B S + I A + + + + +
+ + T W + P + + T + T + W + T A H + + +
+ + + + R + + O + + + E + E + + W + + +
+ + + + + E L + + + + K + A E + + + +
+ + + + + C D E V E E L S C A T + + + +
+ + + + + + + N + + + + R A + E + + +
+ + + + + + + + U + + + + + J + R + +
```

belt, boot, button, clothes, clothing, coat, collar, dress, glove, hat, jacket, jeans, outfit, pocket, scarf, shirt, shoe, skirt, sleeve, suit, sweater, underwear, uniform, wear

Body
(page 202)

```
+ + + + + R + B + + + + + + N W A J +
M + + + N E T A + + + + + + + E + + +
+ O + + I D E C + + + + + + + C + +
+ + U + E L E K + B M U H T N + + + K +
+ + + T V U T + + + G + + + + O + + +
D N A H H O H + + + + E + + + + S + + +
+ + + + + H + + + E C S L + + + R E + +
+ + + + + S + + U H + M T + + I + F + +
+ + + + E + + G E + + R + S A + O + + +
+ + + Y S + N S + + + A + H I O + + S +
+ + E M + O T + + + + + + + T R E + K +
+ + U + T S P I N E + + + + + + W E I +
+ G H E A D + + + + + + L U N G + + N +
+ + + + + + + + + + + + + + + + + + K
+ + + + + + + + + + + + + + + + + + +
```

arms, back, chest, eye, foot, gums, hair, hand, head, jaw, knee, leg, lung, mouth, neck, nose, shoulder, skin, spine, teeth, thumb, tongue, vein, wrist

Fruit
(page 203)

```
W + P G N A + + S + + + + E + G H I
+ A I A V O + + T + + B + + N + R C W
+ F T A P O M R E L P P A E N I P A A I
+ + U E R A A E R A E P N + + R + P E K
+ G + A R W Y + L + + + A + + A + E P +
+ + N + B M + A + + + N + + T L F + +
+ G + E + + E + + + Y S A + + C I R + +
E + R + + + L + A E R + + + E M U + +
+ R + + + + + O I P + R + + N E I + +
Y + + + + + + R N + P E + + + T + +
B L U E B E R R I E S + L + B + + + +
+ + + + + + E + M A N G O E + P + + P +
+ + + + + H G R A P E S + + T + S L + +
+ E E H C Y L + + + + + + + + A U A + +
+ + + + + + + + + + + + + + + M D + R +
```

apple, bananas, blueberries, cherries, date, fig, grapefruit, grapes, guava, kiwi, lemon, lime, lychee, mango, nectarine, orange, papaya, peach, pear, pineapple, plum, raspberry, strawberry, watermelon

Chapter Three — Solutions — Transcriptions

Vegetable
(page 204)

```
+ + N + + + + E + O + + + + B + S C E +
+ + + R + + G L E T T U C E H P + A L +
T + + O A + P E A S + E S R + + U A +
+ U + T B C + + + T + T I O + + + L K +
+ + R B N + I + + O S D U + + B + I + +
+ + A N + A + L + P A T B + + E + F + +
+ C + + I + L + R R S R P + + A + L + S
+ + + + P + P + A O I Y E + N + O + P
R E B M U C U C G C G N + A P S + W + I
S Q U A S H + P C G + I + + M P + E + N
T O R R A C L O + + E H + + + + E R + A
+ + + + + E L + + + + C N O I N O R + C
+ + + + + K I + + + + + C + + + + + S H
+ + + + + + + + + + + + + U + + + + + +
+ + + + + + + + + + + + Z + + + + + + +
```

beans, beets, broccoli, cabbage, carrot, cauliflower, corn, cucumber, eggplant, garlic, kale, kelp, lettuce, onion, peas, peppers, potato, radish, spinach, sprouts, squash, turnip, yam, zucchini

Animal
(page 205)

```
T + + + E E R + F D + + + S + + + E P R
O + + L L T + A + R O + + N + + + L E +
A + A T + U I + E + O N + A + + G E E F
D H R + + R A B G B E G K K + I D P H L
W U + + + K + L B O + S + E R + + H S O
T + T I G E R + L A D + U A Y G O A T W
+ + + + + Y C + + I R + F O + D + N + +
G I P + + A + + + G F + + M R + T + +
+ + + + T + + + + + E A R + + A + + + +
+ + + + + + + + + + + H T + + Z + + + +
+ + + + + + + + + + + I + M O + I + + B
M O N K E Y + + + N + + + O R L + + I +
N E K C I H C W O E S R O H O + + R + +
N O I L + + + O + + + + + + + S D + + +
+ + + + + + + C + + + + + + + + E + + +
```

alligator, bear, bird, cat, chicken, cow, deer, dog, donkey, elephant, frog, giraffe, goat, horse, lion, lizard, monkey, moose, mouse, pig, rabbit, rhino, sheep, snake, tiger, toad, turkey, turtle, whale, wolf

School Words
(page 206)

```
G E O G R A P H Y R R H + + + S + K + P
H I S T O R Y D A E L O + S + T + O H M
+ + + + + + R M T + I M + + E U + O + U
+ + + + + A M H + + C E + + + D N B + S
+ + + + O A G A + + N W S + + E A K + I
+ + + B R I + + L + E O + C T N + R + C
+ + + G L + + + + P P R + I I T T O G N
+ + + H + + + + + E + H K C + + E W + E
+ G + + + + + + + L + A + + A + N + + P
+ I G N I L L E P S B R B C + + + C + +
H + + + + B + + + + U A H E S M A X E +
R E S A R E O + + L + E L T T B O O K S
+ + + + + + + R E + R + + L A + + + + +
+ + + + + + + R E + + + + + Y M + + + +
+ + + + + + + D + + + + + S + + + +
```

alphabet, board, books, bored, eraser, geography, grades, grammar, highlighter, history, homework, math, music, pen, pencil, phonetic, ruler, science, spelling, student, syllable, teacher, exams, workbook

Science
(page 207)

```
+ N + K + + Q + + V + F + S C I S Y H P
+ + O + R U + + + + E + O + E C A P S A
+ T + R A A + + + + T N + R + + T + P T
+ + E N T + U O + E + + U + M + E + R A
+ + T L + C R Q N + + + + S + U L + I D
+ U + + E G E A S T R O N A U T L + S +
M N + + A S L L N + + + Y + + + I A M +
+ + O N + P C E E + R + + + T + + +
+ + I T E + M O E L U C E L O M E S M +
+ S + A O I + + P C + + C + + + + U E +
M + R + R R + + R E + + L + + + + E T +
+ T + E + + P E + + + + I + + + L S +
H + P E L E M E N T + + P + + + C Y +
+ X G A L A X Y + + + + S + + + U S +
E + + + + + + + + + + + E + + + N + +
```

astronaut, data, earth, eclipse, electron, element, experiment, formula, galaxy, mercury, molecule, nucleus, organism, physics, planet, prism, proton, quantum, quark, satellite, space, system, telescope, Venus

Environment
(page 208)

```
+ E + + + N + + + E + G + + + H N H
+ N + + + + O + + V + + A + + + T A A +
+ A O Z O N E I R + T J R + + R T B + +
+ C + + + E E T H + U B + A U I T + +
+ I + + + S X G U + N A E R T E + + +
+ R + + G N + U T + L G G E A M + + + +
O R E C O L O G Y I + L E T P + + + + +
D U E C + R O + T + N E O E L C Y C E R
A H C H D + + B + E + C R P F U T U R E
N + U + T + + + A + N A T N E G Y X O +
R R D + + A + + L T A + + + + + S + +
O + E + + + E + + U + + L + + + + O + +
T + R U + + + W R + + + + P + + L + +
+ + + + S + + E S L A C I M E H C A + +
+ + + + + E + + + + + + + + + + R + +
```

chemicals, conserve, drought, earth, ecology, extinct, future, garbage, global, habitat, hurricane, jungle, nature, oxygen, ozone, planet, pollution, recycle, reduce, reuse, solar, temperature, tornado, weather

Medical
(page 209)

```
C + P + + + + L + + + + Y N H + + A D
+ O + R + + A T + + + + R A G + + B I
+ + N + A C + + N C U R E E I U + + D G
+ E + S I C Y G R E L L A G C O + + O E
R + H S C E T + N E M + + R I C + + M S
+ O Y T S I A I G E O T + U T + + + E T
+ H T R A I O A C P E + N S P + + R N I
P + U C L E S U E E + D S I O + + E + O
+ N + M O S R R S + + N L + O + + M N
+ + E + A D A B + + E + W E L L N E S S
+ N + M + T A R T E R Y + + + + D + +
T + + + I + + Z N O I S I V + + Y +
+ + + O + + + E + + + + + + + + + + +
+ + N + + + + + + + + + + + + + + +
+ + L A T I P S O H + + + + + + + + +
```

abdomen, ailment, allergy, artery, breathe, conscious, cough, cure, digestion, doctor, hospital, massage, needle, nurse, ointment, operation, optician, physical, practice, remedy, sneeze

Workplace
(page 210)

```
P E + W M + + + R A C N T Y + S + + I +
L M + E A A + + U E G O P E E + + + N +
U U + I N + N T + I T O M R K + + + T +
M S + V U + O A E + C N V P + R + + E +
B E + R F M + R G O + I E + U + A + R +
E R + E A + O + T E C + + P + T + M E Y
R + + T C F + O + E R + + + R + E M S M
+ + I N T Y H B E N E F I T S A P R T O
+ O + I U P N + T R O P X E + L C Y + N
N + + R + + A + S + + + O + R + + O
+ + + + E + + + P + H + + Y + A + + + C
T N U O C C A + + M + I E + L + + + + E
+ + + + + + + + + + O E F A R E T I R E
N A I C I N H C E T + C S T + + + + + +
+ + + + + + + + + + + + F O R E M A N
```

account, automation, benefits, carpenter, company, computer, economy, employee, export, foreign, foreman, interest, interview, manager, manufacture, market, photocopy, plumber, resume, retire, salary, service, shift, technician

Line Match Grammar Words
(page 211)

Verb: to be I'm – time, you're – floor, he's – freeze or please, she's – freeze or please, we're – clear, they're – stair, were – sir

Future I'll – style, he'll – steel, meal or wheel, she'll – steel, meal or wheel, we'll – steel, meal or wheel, you'll – cool, they'll – nail

Line Match Ordinary Words
(page 212)

does /duz/- **buzz** /buz/, **said** /sed/- **red** /red/, **half** /haf/- **laugh** /laf/, **busy** /bizɛy/- **Is he?**/izɛy/, **quite**/kwɪyt/ - **right** /rɪyt/, **talk** /tok/ - **rock** /rok/, **Mrs.** /misiz/ - **misses** /misiz/. **of** /uv/ - **love** /luv/, **suit** /sʊwt/ - **boot** /bʊwt/, **eight** /ʌyt/ - **great** /grʌyt/, **through** /THrʊw/ - **you** /yʊw/, **Mr.** /misdɛr/- **sister** /sisdɛr/, **was** /wuz/ - **fuzz** /fuz/, **child** /chɪyld/ - **wild** /wɪyld/, **drawer** /drɔr/ - **or**/ɔr/, **enough** /ɛynuf/ - **stuff** /stuf/, **lose** /lʊwz/ - **news** /nʊwz/, **young** /yuNg/ - **sung** /suNg/, **quiet** /kwɪyet/, **sew** /sɔw/ - **go** /gɔw/

References

Books

Nilsen, D.L.F., & Nilsen, A.P. (1973). *Pronunciation Contrasts in English*, Englewood Cliffs, NJ: Prentice Hall Regents

Pierce, T. (2005), *Greatest Goofiest Jokes*, New York: Sterling Publishing Co., Inc.

Thompson, J. (2009), *English is Stupid*, Caledon, ON: Thompson Language Center

Media

http://puzzlemaker.discoveryeducation.com/WordSearchSetupForm.asp

www.youtube.com
  My Fair Lady, The Rain in Spain,
    http://www.youtube.com/watch?v=uVmU3iANbgk
  Bingo Song, http://www.youtube.com/watch?v=KUDZiu_SVzw

JUDY THOMPSON, B.A. English, TESL, Pronunciation Expert, Author, TEDx speaker has been educating students and teachers for over 25 years. A venerate pattern-thinker dissatisfied with industrial education, Judy approaches learning differently. Paring English conversation down to simple rules with no exceptions, was a watershed moment. Judy's pattern-based, learn-by-doing model for English conversation works for students of all levels and has been embraced by progressive teachers in over 60 countries.

NOTES

NOTES

NOTES

NOTES

Thompson Language Center
PRODUCT LIST

English is Crazy — the definitive speaking guide
An innovative working textbook for the fastest method for learning to speak English ever developed. Speaking isn't writing said out loud.

The English Phonetic Alphabet Workbook — over 200 pronunciation activities
Companion to Chapter One of **English is Crazy** – these exercises to instil the 40 sounds of the English language, suitable for Basic to Advanced learners.

Speaking Made Simple — Course Curriculum
A stand-alone, step by step, 360 page speaking course based on the patterns of spoken English introduced in **English is Crazy**. Treasured by a wide range of ESL/EFL institutions worldwide since 2011.

How Do You Say? — Spelling, Pronunciation and Expressions Dictionary
The 2,000 most common words in English organized by main vowel sound from the *Thompson Vowel Chart* featured in **English is Crazy**. Easy access to how words are spelled, what they mean, how they are pronounced, and how they are used in expressions. Learners LOVE it.

Backpacker's Guide to Teaching English
— for casual instructors with no **previous training** or **experience**

BOOK 1 **Cracking the Code** – on Pronunciation
BOOK 2 **Need For Speed** – on Conversation
BOOK 3 **You Don't Say** – on Fluency

ABC Facilitated Reading - An interactive literacy system for learning to read at home
This revolutionary program effectively addresses crazy English spelling in a simple, interactive process parents and leaners enjoy. **Facilitated learning** in general evokes security, creativity, confidence, inclusion, relationship, life-skills, and fun.

A range of educational Poster and Flashcard PDFs are available from
www.thompsonlanguagecenter.com

For more information or to order products, contact judy@thompsonlanguagecenter.com

Changing the way the world learns

www.ingramcontent.com/pod-product-compliance
Lightning Source LLC
Chambersburg PA
CBHW081215230426
43666CB00015B/2731